# The Babes in the Wood

A pantomime

# Norman Robbins

Samuel French — London
New York - Toronto - Hollywood

# CHARACTERS
*(in order of appearance)*

The **Bailiff** of Nottingham
The **Sheriff** of Nottingham
**Jill** and **Jack,** the Babes
**Nurse Glucose,** their Nanny
**Robin Hood**
**Toyle** and **Trubble,** two would-be villains
**Maid Marion,** the Sheriff's Ward
The Woodland **Fairy**
**Friar Tuck**
**Will Scarlett**
**Much,** the Miller's son
**Alan a-Dale**
A **Ghost**

Chorus of Citizens, Merry Men, Toys, etc.
Junior Chorus of Children, Toys, Birds, etc.

# SYNOPSIS OF SCENES

## ACT I

## ACT II

# MUSIC

The choice of songs is left to the individual director. However, Norman Robbins has prepared a list of suggested songs, which is available upon request from Samuel French Ltd.

A licence issued by Samuel French Ltd to perform this play does not include permission to use any copyright music in the performance. Where the place of performance is already licensed by the Performing Right Society a return of the music used must be made to them. If the place of performance is not so licensed then application should be made to the PERFORMING RIGHT SOCIETY, 29 Berners Street, London W1.

A separate and additional licence from PHONOGRAPHIC PERFORMANCES LTD, Ganton House, Ganton Street, London W1, is needed whenever commercial recordings are used.

## AUTHOR'S NOTE

Although I've appeared professionally in several versions of *Babes in the Wood*, it's never been one of my favourites, so I had no particular urge to write a version of my own. To begin with, it's really two pantomimes rolled into one: the original "Babes in the Wood" (based on the true-life murder of two children in Norfolk's Wayland Wood by their wicked uncle about five hundred years ago), and the pantomime "Robin Hood", which were joined together around 1795 and, to my mind, have rested uneasily together ever since. Also I have painful memories of a production in the late 1960s which left me bruised and limping for several weeks.

However, in 1993 I was approached by Newton Abbot Young Farmers to write them a forty-minute version of "Babes" for their National Pantomime Competition, which promptly carried them past 363 rival teams and into the Finals at Blackpool Opera House, collecting several awards on the way. One member of the judging panel was so impressed with their effort, she asked me to expand the version to full length which would enable her local amateur group to perform it. In 1994, this played with outstanding success and prompted a flurry of enquiries as to its availability for other groups. Having now deleted the specific requests of the Society concerned for this version, I offer it for your appreciation. As usual, staging should cause little problem. Each full-set scene is followed by a lane-cloth scene, lighting is simple and props minimal. Just keep the music bright and the pace lively, and a good time should be had by all.

Norman Robbins

For John and Carole
(As a reminder of those Babes on Hook Moor)

# ACT I

## Scene 1

*Old Nottingham. A bright sunny morning*

*The backdrop is a typical pantomime setting of half-timbered and thatched cottages, with thick forest in the background. A glimpse of Nottingham Castle could perhaps be seen* UL. *A bakery or inn stands* L *and a sweetshop is* R. *These mask entrances and exits*

*When the* Curtain *rises the Citizens and their Children are singing and dancing happily*

### Song 1: Citizens and Children

*At the end of the song the Bailiff enters* UL, *rudely pushing his way through the Crowd*

**Bailiff** (*loudly*) Make way for the Sheriff. The Sheriff of Nottingham.

*He continues* DR *to stand as the Crowd reluctantly move aside to leave a clear entrance for the Sheriff*

*The Sheriff enters* UL *and moves* DC. *He is more of a would-be villain than an actual one, full of bluster, but quite cowardly when faced with someone who will hit back. He carries a rolled scroll and has a self-satisfied sneer on his face*

**Sheriff** (*grandly*) Three cheers for me. Hip, hip ...
**Crowd** (*loudly*) Boo.
**Sheriff** (*annoyed*) Silence, you nuciferous numbskulls. How dare you raise your voices to me? (*Importantly*) I bring a message from His Royal Highness, Prince John — Ruler of all England.
**Citizen 1** (*loudly*) Rubbish. Richard the Lionheart rules England. Prince John's nothing but a coward who stays at home in safety whilst our real King fights in the Holy Crusades.

*All agree noisily*

**Sheriff** (*stung*) Enough. One more word and I'll have you all thrown into the castle dungeons.

*The Crowd fall silent*

(*Growling*) So ... this is what I get for being gentle and kind-hearted, is it? Very well. From this moment on, things are going to change. (*Firmly*) I am revolting. (*He strikes an attitude*)
**Citizen 2** (*disdainfully*) We already know that.

*The Crowd laugh*

**Sheriff** (*annoyed*) Who said that? Who said that? (*He glares at them*)

*No-one speaks*

(*Snapping*) Bailiff!

*The Bailiff approaches him*

Read this proclamation.(*He hands the scroll to the Bailiff*)
**Bailiff** (*unrolling the scroll and reading loudly*) By permission of His Royal Highness, Prince John ... any person giving information leading to the arrest of the outlaw Robin Hood and his band of Merry Men, shall be given fifty pieces of gold. Signed, Cedric Spindleshanks, Sheriff of Nottingham. (*He rolls up the scroll again*)
**Sheriff** (*sneering*) Now then. Who wants to claim the reward, eh? Don't all speak at once.
**Citizen 3** (*disgustedly*) If you think we'll betray Robin Hood, my Lord Sheriff, then you'd better think again. You can keep your measly reward.

*All agree and turn away*

**Sheriff** (*spluttering*) But it's a Royal Decree.
**Citizen 1** (*turning back*) Royal Decree, my foot. It's not Prince John who wants Robin Hood out of the way. It's you. You'd do anything to keep him away from Lady Marion.

*All agree*

**Sheriff** (*defensively*) And why shouldn't I? No ward of mine is going to marry a common outlaw. She's far too beautiful for the likes of him. (*Harshly*) Now clear off, you scrofulous scraps of scorbutic sarcoid. And remember this. If I catch any of you helping Robin Hood, it's the gallows for everyone.

*The Crowd jeer derisively and exit variously*

(*Glowering*) I'll show those pusillanimous peasants who's boss around here. Whether they like it or not, Robin Hood and his gang will soon be hanging from the highest oak in Sherwood Forest.

*He exits* DL, *followed by the Bailiff. As he does so, Jack and Jill enter* UR. *Jill is seven years old and Jack is nine. Both are dressed neatly for travelling*

**Jill** (*running* DC) Wheeeeeeeee. We're here. We're here. (*She twirls around*)
**Jack** (*following her down*) Look at all the funny houses. It's not a bit like Lincoln, is it?
**Jill** (*gazing around*) Oh, Jack! There's a stables ... and a baker's ... and a toyshop and ... look ... a sweetshop. (*She hurries to it*)
**Jack** It's no use looking in there, Jill. You know Nursie won't let us have any more. We had a whole bagful of humbugs on the journey.
**Jill** (*disappointedly*) I know. (*She turns to him*) But I'm still hungry, aren't you?
**Jack** Starving.
**Jill** And where is Nursie, anyway?
**Nurse** (*off* R) Yoo-hoo. Children? Are you there, dears?
**Jack** (*looking* UR) Here she comes now.

*Nurse Glucose enters* UR *in full travelling outfit and laden down with assorted bags, suitcases, packages and umbrella, etc. She totters* DC, *gasping for breath*

**Nurse** Oooooh. Somebody give me a hand. I think I've pulled a trunion.

*The Babes help her lower the bags, etc.*

Thank goodness for that. Another minute and I'd have had a mid-life crisis and a sagging undercarriage. (*Crossly*) What did you want to go running off like that for, you naughty children? I nearly had a conniption.

**Jill** (*contrite*) Sorry, Nurse Glucose. (*Eagerly*) But is this where we're going to live? Really and truly?

**Nurse** (*mollified*) That's right, dear. In a great big castle with your nice kind Uncle Cedric.

**Jack** (*unhappily*) Do we have to?

**Nurse** (*surprised*) Well, of course you do, dear. Now your poor father's dead, where else can you go?

**Jack** (*protesting*) But we've never even met Uncle Cedric. What if we don't like him?

**Nurse** Oh, you don't want to worry about that. If he's anything like your father was, he'll be debonair, suave, tall, dark ... and hands. (*She remembers herself*) I mean handsome. (*She clears her throat*) Now come along. We don't want to be late, do we?

**Jack** But are you sure he's expecting us?

**Nurse** Well, of course he is. Your father sent him a letter just before he died. All in joined up writing. (*To the audience*) It's a wonderful thing, isn't it? Education. (*To the Babes*) And I posted it myself with a first-class stamp on it. Seventy-five pence. (*She looks pleased*)

**Jill** But a first-class stamp is only (*she names the cost*), Nurse Glucose.

**Nurse** (*startled*) Is it? (*Stricken*) Oh, no. That means it'll have gone too far. (*Brightening*) Still ... never mind. I'm sure he'll be pleased to see us.

**Jack** (*dolefully*) Which way do we go, then?

**Nurse** (*stumped*) I haven't a clue. But never mind. Leave everything to dear old Nursie. She'll find out. You go look at the ducks on the pond over there (*she indicates off* DL) while I have a chat with this lot down here in the sewer ... (*quickly*) I mean the auditorium. (*She beams at the audience*) One of them's bound to know the way.

**Jack** All right. But please don't be too long, Nursie. We're absolutely starving. (*To Jill*) Come on, Jill.

*Jack and Jill exit* DL

**Nurse** (*to the audience*) Now then. Let's have a look at you. (*She peers at them*) Oooh, I say. Aren't you a bonny looking lot? (*She hesitates*) Well all except that woman over there. (*She indicates vaguely*) She's got ever such a funny look on her face. (*To her*) Excuse me, love ... Are you sure you're sitting the right way up? (*She chuckles*) Well, I'd better introduce meself, hadn't I? Glucose is the name. Nurse Glucose ... and I look after those two charming children you saw just a minute ago. Mind you ... what a time I've had getting them here. We had to come all the way from Lincoln on the bus. And talk about crowded. It was so full even the men were standing. I thought, "Oh, dear. I can't stand all the way to Nottingham. Me feet are killing me. Whatever can I do to get a seat?" And then I thought, "I know. I'll use a bit of sex appeal." So I looked at this feller sitting nearest to me (*she indicates*) over here ... ever so good-looking, he was ... and I gave him a wink. Like this. (*She demonstrates*) Well he didn't take a blind bit of notice, but the feller next to him started to get to his feet. Well I didn't want his seat. He had a face like a bottle of warts. So I pushed him back down and said, "It's all right, love. I'm a liberated woman. I can stand." But talk about persistent! Two seconds later he's on his feet again and trying to get out. I thought "Honestly. Some people. They just can't take a hint, can they?", and I shoved him down again. "It's all right," I said. "I've already told you. I don't mind standing." Well ... I think he was a bit peculiar, because the minute I'd turned me back, he was up again. So I turned round and I said, "Listen, mush. I've already told you twice. I don't want your seat. Now sit down and stop embarrassing me." Well ... he went red as a beetroot and said, "I'm sorry, madam, but you'll have to let me get up. I've already gone ten stops past my getting-off place." (*She chuckles*) Mind you ... you meet some funny people on buses, don't you? Well, I do. There was a feller sitting at the back and ——

*Robin Hood enters* UR *and moves* DC. *He is a dashing young man, dressed as a forester in Lincoln green*

**Robin** (*brightly*) Good-morning!
**Nurse** (*turning to him*) Good heavens — it's (*she names a young pop star*)!
**Robin** (*amused*) I'm afraid not. Robin Hood, at your service, ma'am. (*He gives a very deep bow*)
**Nurse** (*to the audience*) Oooh, I say ... The last feller I saw with his head that low was looking for a lost contact lens. Play me cards right, and I could be in with a chance, here. (*To Robin*) Eczema Glucose ... Children's Nurse and Spinster of this Parish. (*She simpers and curtsies*)
**Robin** (*blinking*) Excuse me? Did you say ... Eczema? That's ... rather an unusual name, isn't it?
**Nurse** Well ... me real name's Mabel, but everybody calls me Eczema because once you get me on your hands, it's hard to get rid of me. (*She laughs, then remembers*) Oh. Here. I say. You don't happen to know where the castle is, do you?
**Robin** Why, yes. It's over there. (*He indicates off* UL)

**Nurse** (*looking*) Oh. Silly old me. We must have walked straight past it. That's the worst thing about being short sighted, you know. You can't see where you're going, half the time.

**Robin** (*politely*) Don't you wear glasses?

**Nurse** Ooooh, I can't afford glasses on my wages, dear.

**Robin** Then why not try carrots? Friar Tuck says they're very good for improving the sight.

**Nurse** Well, don't you believe him. I tried them once, and they don't half hurt when you stick 'em in your eyes.

**Robin** (*laughing, then changing the subject*) So you're looking for the Sheriff of Nottingham, are you?

**Nurse** That's right, dear. I've brought his little niece and nephew to live with him, and they're so anxious to meet him, you wouldn't believe it.

**Robin** Well, let's hope they won't be too disappointed when they do. He's not the nicest man you're likely to meet here. Most people wouldn't trust him as far as they could throw him.

**Nurse** (*worried*) Oh, I say. (*Anxiously*) They are going to be all right with him, aren't they? I mean ... he will take care of them?

**Robin** (*quickly*) Oh, I'm sure he will. After all ... he's looked after Marion since she was a child.

**Nurse** (*relieved*) Oh, that's all right then. (*Curiously*) Who's Marion?

**Robin** Lady Marion Fitzherbert, his ward. The most wonderful girl in the world, and hopefully, the one I'm going to marry.

**Nurse** (*archly*) Oooh, I say. It's like that, is it? Wedding bells in the air. I like a good wedding meself, you know. Oh, yes. Only last week I went to a wooden wedding.

**Robin** (*puzzled*) Wooden wedding?

**Nurse** That's right, dear. My best friend married a blockhead.

*She laughs, pushes him playfully and sends him flying*

Here ... I say. And while we're on the subject, I ... er ... I don't suppose there's any spare fellers living around this place, are there?

**Robin** Oh, I'm sure you'll find lots of admirers once you've settled in. It's a very friendly city.

**Nurse** (*delightedly*) Oooh, I can hardly wait to start fighting them off. (*She remembers*) Here ... and speaking of settling in ... I'd better get the children up to the castle. They've got to be all freshened up before I introduce them to their uncle. (*She calls* DL) Jack. Jill.

*Jack and Jill enter DL*

Come and meet our first new friend here ... Mr Robin Hood.

**Babes** Hallo.
**Robin** (*warmly*) Hallo, children.

*He shakes hands with them*

Welcome to Nottingham. And I hope you'll all be very happy here.
**Jack** Well we'll do our best, I suppose. And at least the forest looks interesting. We can't wait to explore it, (*to Jill*) can we, Jill?
**Robin** (*hastily*) Oh, I don't think that's a good idea, Jack. Not by yourselves, anyway. It's full of wolves and other wild animals.

*The Babes look disappointed*

But I'll tell you what. Whenever you feel you'd like to have a look round, just give me a call and I'll show you all the nice places.
**Jill** (*eagerly*) Honest and truly?
**Robin** Honest and truly. After all ... if we're going to be friends, then it's the very least I can do, isn't it?

## Song 2: Robin, Nurse and Babes

*If required, the Citizens may also enter and join in the second chorus of the song*

*At the end of it, Robin exits* UR *waving. Nurse and the Babes pick up their luggage and exit* UL. *Citizens exit* L *and* R

*A moment later, Toyle and Trubble enter* UR *and move* DC. *They are dressed in grubby leather jerkins, balloon-sleeved shirts, cavalier boots and baggy trousers. Trubble also wears a battered, floppy-brimmed hat. Both are armed with pistols*

**Toyle** (*glancing around*) Here we are, Trubble. Nottingham at last. Let's hope we have better luck here than we did in (*local town or district*).
**Trubble** (*disgustedly*) Yes. You can certainly say that again, Toyle. It was the first time I'd seen a cemetery with shops and street lights. Anyway ... this looks a bit more promising. We'll soon find a job here. (*He looks around with interest*)
**Toyle** What do you mean, "We'll soon find a job here"? We've got a job.
**Trubble** (*blankly*) Have we?
**Toyle** Of course we have. (*Firmly*) We're robbers.
**Trubble** Robbers?

**Toyle** (*facing the audience*) Brigands.

**Trubble** Brigands?

**Toyle** (*proudly*) Footpads. (*He strikes an attitude*)

**Trubble** (*decisively*) Shin pads.

**Toyle** (*fiercely*) Highwaymen.

**Trubble** (*getting carried away*) Low-way men.

**Toyle** Tough and ruthless.

**Trubble** (*almost deliriously*) Rough and toothless.

**Toyle** (*realizing*) Idiot. (*He pushes him in annoyance*)

**Trubble** (*indignantly*) Here ... who are you calling an idiot? I've got an IQ of seven, I have.

**Toyle** (*amazed*) IQ of seven? But that's pathetic.

**Trubble** I know. But it's six more than anybody in the (*local Planning Department*)

**Toyle** (*exasperated*) What's the matter with you this morning? Come on. Spit it out. You've done nothing but look miserable ever since you got up.

**Trubble** (*squirming*) Well ... I'm fed up with being a robber.

**Toyle** (*amazed*) Fed up with being a ro— How can you possibly be fed up with being a robber? Look at you. You've never done an honest day's work in your life. You make your living by stealing other people's hard-earned money. You're selfish, tight-fisted and riddled with corruption. You never listen to reason, and you haven't used your brain in years. What other sort of job could you get with those qualifications?

**Trubble** (*after a moment's thought*) I could work for the Inland Revenue.

**Toyle** (*wincing*) All right. All right. Just suppose for one minute that you could find another kind of job. What is it you'd really like to do?

**Trubble** (*thinking furiously*) Er ... er ... (*he decides*) be a comedian.

**Toyle** (*incredulously*) A comedian? (*He bursts out laughing*)

**Trubble** (*blankly*) What? What?

**Toyle** You couldn't be a comedian, you fathead. It's not easy to make people laugh, you know.

**Trubble** It is if you play for (*local football or rugby team*). (*He chortles*)

**Toyle** (*annoyed*) I might have expected a stupid remark like that from you. But you don't fool me, you know. I know why you don't want to be a robber anymore. It's because you're a coward, isn't it? A low-down, yellow-livered, craven coward.

**Trubble** (*stung*) Just a minute, you. Just a minute. For your information, I come from a family of world-famous fighters, I do. One of my ancestors conquered half the world.

**Toyle** (*impressed*) Blimey. I didn't know that.
**Trubble** He'd have conquered the other half, as well, if somebody hadn't
   taken his conkers away. (*He chortles*)
**Toyle** (*annoyed*) Ooooh.

*He snatches Trubble's hat and begins to beat him around the head and
shoulders with it*

**Trubble** Owwwwwww.
**Toyle** (*thrusting the hat back at him*) Now stop messing about and let's
   find somebody to rob. If we don't get some money soon, we're going
   to starve to death.

*Maid Marion enters* UL, *moving slowly* DC. *She carries a large envelope
and is studying the writing on it, a puzzled look on her face*

**Trubble** (*seeing her*) Cor. What a smasher. I bet she's got a penny or two.
**Toyle** Not half. Come on. Let's rob her before she gets away.

*Trubble quickly puts his hat on and they creep over and seize her*

   (*Harshly*) Hand over your cash.
**Marion** (*startled*) Help! Help! (*She drops the letter*)

*Robin enters* UR

**Robin** (*seeing the struggle*) What? (*He hurries down and grabs Toyle*)
   Take that. (*He punches him*)

*As Toyle howls, Robin grabs Trubble and gives him the same treatment*

   *With much howling, the Robbers exit* UL

   Marion. Are you all right?

*He embraces her*

**Marion** Oh, Robin. Thank goodness you arrived in time. (*Dismayed*) But
   what are you doing here? Don't you know Prince John's put a price on
   your head? Fifty gold pieces to anyone who'll betray you.
**Robin** (*amused*) I don't think he'll find many takers in this city. But even
   if he did, I couldn't keep away. Not while you're here.

**Marion**  All the same, I'd feel a lot happier if I knew you were safe in Sherwood Forest. Uncle Cedric's sworn to catch you if it's the last thing he does.

**Robin**  (*lightly*) Well, I'll just have to take my chances, won't I? But don't worry, Marion. I only came into Nottingham to invite you to dine with us tonight. We'll be feasting beneath the greenwood tree and we'd be honoured if you'd care to join us. Of course ... we don't have fine chairs and tables, or even knives and forks ... but we do have the best venison you've ever tasted and the company's the merriest in England.

**Marion**  (*happily*) Then what more could anyone ask for? Except the return of King Richard from the Crusades to make you a free man again.

**Robin**  (*wistfully*) One day, perhaps. (*He brightens*) But until then, I don't mind being an outlaw if I know you still believe in me.

**Marion**  You know I do. And I always will.

### Song 3: Robin and Marion

*At the end of the song, Marion glances off* L *and gives a startled gasp*

Uncle Cedric. And he's heading this way.

*She tries to hurry Robin off* R

**Robin**  (*remembering*) But I've got some other news for you, too. You'll never believe this, but ——

**Marion**  (*still pushing him*) Tell me tonight.

**Robin**  (*protesting*) But ——

**Marion**  (*urgently*) Tonight. (*She pushes him off* R)

*Robin exits* R *reluctantly. As he does so, the Sheriff enters* L

**Sheriff**  (*smarmily*) Ah, Marion, my dear. I've been looking for you everywhere.

**Marion**  (*innocently*) And I've been looking for you. (*She picks up the letter she dropped*) This letter's just arrived at the castle. From Lincoln. (*She holds it out to him*)

**Sheriff**  (*opening his eyes*) Lincoln? But the only person I know in Lincoln is that pious brother of mine. (*He snatches the letter and looks at the writing*) Yes. That's his writing. What on earth does he want? (*He opens the envelope, extracts the letter and reads aloud*) "My dear Cedric ... Alas, I am dying and my two sweet children, Jack and Jill, will soon have no-one to care for them. I beg you to shelter them, cherish them as your own ... and see that their fortune is invested wisely. Your loving brother, Alfrick." (*Outraged*) What? Me look after children? Never. I hate children. Loathe children. Despise children. And besides ... why didn't he leave his fortune to me instead of to a pair of snivelling brats who'll spent it all on video games and other such rubbish? No wonder I always disliked him. (*Grimly*) Well if he thinks I'm going to look after them, he can jolly well think again.

**Marion**  (*quickly*) Oh, but Uncle ... To have children in the castle. It's about time we had some laughter in that gloomy old place.

**Sheriff**  (*firmly*) Never. Over my dead body.

*Nurse enters* DL, *as before, with luggage*

**Nurse**  (*calling over her shoulder*) This way, children. This way. (*She stops and looks around*) Oh ... We must have taken a wrong turning. We're back where we started from. (*She sees the Sheriff and Marion*) I'd better ask the way again. (*She drops the baggage and taps the Sheriff's shoulder*) Excuse me.

**Sheriff**  (*turning in annoyance*) Yes?

**Nurse**  (*reacting*) Blimey. Is it Hallowe'en already?

**Sheriff**  (*snarling*) What do you want?

**Nurse**  (*recovering herself*) Well ... I'm looking for the Sheriff of Nottingham. To give him a nice surprise.

**Sheriff**  (*suspiciously*) Surprise? You're not a Kiss-o-gram Granny, are you?

**Nurse**  (*taken aback*) Certainly not.

**Sheriff**  (*rudely*) Very well then. Hand it over and clear off. (*He extends his hand*)

**Nurse**  (*indignantly*) It's not an it. It's a them. And why should I hand them over to you?

**Sheriff**  Because I'm the Sheriff, you flannel-faced old faggot. Can't you tell by my deportment? (*He puffs himself up and strikes a pose*)

**Nurse**  (*impressed*) Oh, I say. I knew a feller once who had deportment lessons. Had 'em for months, he did.

**Sheriff**  (*snootily*) Really? And did they work?

**Nurse**  Oh, yes. The day after he finished 'em, he got deported.

*She laughs and slaps the Sheriff's back, sending him flying*

*The Babes enter* DL, *carrying a large money bag*

**Jack**  (*wearily*) Aren't we there yet, Nurse Glucose?

**Jill**  This bag's awfully heavy.

**Nurse** (*beaming*) Never mind, dears. Just drop it there and say hallo to your nice, kind Uncle Cedric.

*The Babes put the bag down*

**Sheriff** (*astounded*) What? (*He looks at them in disbelief*)
**Marion** (*delightedly*) You mean ... this is Jack and Jill?
**Nurse** That's right, dear. And I'm Nurse Glucose. (*Puzzled*) But who are you?
**Marion** (*warmly*) Maid Marion. The Sheriff's other ward.
**Nurse** (*pleased*) Oh, I say. You're the one who's going to marry that nice Robin Hood, aren't you? Yes. Well ... it's nothing to do with me, dear ... but are you quite sure you're not making a big mistake?
**Marion** (*surprised*) Mistake?
**Nurse** (*brightly*) Well, there's not many girls would want to marry a feller who wears high-heeled shoes, fishnet tights and lipstick. (*She beams*) Still ... if somebody would like to take us to the castle, I'll get everything unpacked then we can all get to know each other before we have lunch. (*She starts collecting her baggage*)
**Sheriff** (*outraged*) Lunch?
**Nurse** (*to the Babes*) And don't forget the bag of gold, dears.
**Sheriff** (*startled*) Gold? (*Eagerly*) Did you say gold?
**Jill** That's right, Uncle Cedric.
**Jack** It's the money Father left us in his will. Fifty thousand pounds.

*The Sheriff's eyes pop and he fights to keep control*

**Sheriff** (*with false geniality*) Well, well, well. It's no wonder you're looking so tired. (*To Marion*) Marion, my dear. Take these beautiful, charming people to the castle and give them something to eat. Don't worry about the luggage. I'll attend to that.
**Marion** (*surprised*) You will? (*She recovers*) Well, in that case ... (*To the Babes and Nurse*) If you'd like to come this way?

*Marion leads them off* UL *and they exit*

*The Sheriff hurries to the money bag and picks it up gleefully*

**Sheriff** Fifty thousand pounds. Fifty thousand pounds. (*He dances around with it*)

*Nurse re-enters* UL

**Nurse** Here, I say. I've just thought on. If you're going to carry the rest of the luggage, I think *I* can manage that. (*She takes the bag from him*) See you back at the castle.

*She beams at him and exits again*

**Sheriff** (*fuming*) Bah. A fortune in gold coins, and only two little babes between me and it. Ooooh ... if only there were some way to swindle them out of it. (*He thinks, then shakes his head*) No, it's no use. That flea-bitten old nurse of theirs will be watching them night and day. (*He begins to gather up the luggage, then pauses*) Still ... now they're living in the castle, I've got plenty of time to work something out. Oh, yes. By this time next week, every penny of it will be mine. All mine. (*He gives a nasty laugh, gathers up the rest of the luggage and sings*) "If I were a rich man ..."

*He exits UL*

*The Lights dim*

*The Fairy enters DR in a white follow spot*

**Fairy** (*watching him go*) Oh, no, my Lord High Sheriff.
　　　　Your schemes will come to naught.
　　　　Just try to cheat those children
　　　　And a lesson sharp I'll see you're taught.
　　　　For years your nasty, wicked, ways
　　　　Have caused me great concern,
　　　　But from now on, 'tis my intent,
　　　　Each plot of yours to overturn.
　　　　Those Babes I promise to protect,
　　　　So better far, be wary,
　　　　For woe betide the mortal who
　　　　Offends the Woodland Fairy.

(*She turns to audience*)

　　　　Fear not, dear friends, no matter what
　　　　Foul deed he may intend,
　　　　I'll be close by to guard the Babes
　　　　And bring this tale to happy end.

*The Fairy exits*

*Cut follow spot and fade to Black-out*

SCENE 2

*A quiet street. Daytime*

*A lane scene. Nurse Glucose enters anxiously from* R

**Nurse**  (*calling*) Yoo-hoo. Children. Are you there, dears? (*To the audience*) Sorry to wake you up, but you haven't seen the Babes anywhere, have you? I only turned my back for a minute, and there they were gone. Ooooh, it didn't half give me a turn. I had to go into the (*local pub*) for a gin and Windolene to steady me nerves. (*To an audience member*) That's right, love. Gin and Windolene. Have you tried it? (*To audience in general*) Doesn't taste very nice, but if you do get drunk, at least your eyes stay bright and sparkling. (*Worried*) Oh, but I wonder where they've got to? I know we've been here two weeks now and they've made lots of friends, but it's not safe in the streets these days, is it? Only last night, a strange feller followed me all down (*local street*) and round the market place. Yes. I walked ever so slowly, but he wouldn't catch up. In the end I complained to a policeman. "Here", I said, "that feller's bothering me." Well the policeman looked him up and down and said, "What are you talking about? He's not even looking at you." I said, "I know. That's what's bothering me." Mind you, he wasn't bad looking himself. And lovely manners. (*Coyly*) Offered to walk me back to the castle. (*Gleefully*) Ooooh, girls. You should have seen us. There we were ... strolling along in the moonlight, eating fish and chips out of his helmet ... when suddenly he turned towards me and asked if I'd like to see where he'd had his operation done. (*She gives a knowing look at the audience*) "Well", I thought, "I'm a woman of this world", so I said "Why not?" (*Pause*) It was the biggest mistake of my life. He took me down this dark alleyway, round a corner and under a railway bridge ... and when there wasn't another soul about ... (*she glances from side to side to make sure she is not being overheard*) he showed it to me. (*She pauses for effect, then continues conversationally*) I'd no idea you could see Nottingham Hospital from there.

*The Sheriff enters from* L

**Sheriff**  A-ha. Nurse Glucose. Just the woman I'm looking for. (*He leers*) I've got a little job for you.
**Nurse**  (*blankly*) Little job?
**Sheriff**  Yes. You've been living in my castle for two weeks now, eating my food and drinking my wines ... and haven't paid me a single penny.

**Nurse** Well how can I? I haven't any money.

**Sheriff** (*triumphantly*) Exactly. So I'm giving you a job. From now on, you'll be Headmistress of Nottingham Incomprehensible School and I'll pay you ten pounds a year. We haven't had a teacher there in ages.

**Nurse** (*indignantly*) Nottingham Incompre—— You must be joking. I'm not working in that place. It's overrun with rats.

**Sheriff** (*off handedly*) Yes. I know. I ... er ... did send one of my servants down to (*local chemist*) to get some rat poison, but unfortunately they'd just sold out.

**Nurse** Well, have you tried Boots?

**Sheriff** I want them poisoning, you old faggot. Not kicked to death. Now off you go, and don't forget. You start work first thing tomorrow morning. Understand?

*Nurse exits* R, *looking doubtful*

(*He gazes after her*) That'll keep her busy for a while. And now to think of a foolproof way of getting my hands on the Babes' money. I've tried hinting and I've tried demanding, but they've outwitted me every time. (*As the thought strikes him*) However ... If something slightly fatal were to happen to the little darlings, then everything would come to me. (*Excitedly*) Yes. Yes. (*He controls himself*) But there must be no suspicion that *I* had a hand in it. What I really need is pair of idiots to assist me. But who? (*He looks off* L) Hallo ... these two look promising. I'll hide and listen to what they're saying.

*He exits* R *as Toyle and Trubble enter from* L

**Trubble** (*gloomily*) Oh, I'm fed up with this lot. We've been here two weeks now, and we still haven't got any money.

**Toyle** Yes. And who's to blame for that, eh? It's you. How do you expect to get rich if you won't get out of bed for days on end?

**Trubble** (*defensively*) It wasn't my fault. I was poorly. I had a bad case of Alice.

**Toyle** Alice? Alice? What on earth's Alice?

**Trubble** I don't know ... but it's the same thing Christopher Robin went down with. (*He laughs*)

**Toyle** (*annoyed*) Ooooh. You know what your trouble is, don't you? You're idle. Bone idle.

**Trubble** (*indignantly*) No, I'm not. I had a real hard job, once. I worked in the (*local snack bar or tea room*).

**Toyle** (*in disbelief*) You? Worked in (*he repeats the name*)? Don't make me laugh.

**Trubble**  It's true. But I got the sack because some stupid woman came
  in and asked for hot chocolate.
**Toyle**  (*puzzled*) How could you get sacked because somebody asked for
  hot chocolate?
**Trubble**  (*grimacing*) I gave her a Yorkie bar and a box of matches.

*Toyle winces and covers his eyes*

  Ooooh. I could just eat a Yorkie bar now, as well. I'm absolutely
  famished.
**Toyle**  Me too. We haven't had a thing to eat for a week. (*He groans*) Oh,
  if only we could win the Football Pools.
**Trubble**  (*brightening*) Here. I had an uncle once who won the Football
  Pools. Two million pounds, he got.
**Toyle**  (*amazed*) Two million pounds? Cor. The lucky thing. (*Suddenly*)
  But what did he do about all the begging letters?
**Trubble**  He kept sending 'em.

*Toyle pushes him in annoyance*

**Toyle**  Look. We've got to get money, somehow. Otherwise we're going
  to starve to death.

  *The Sheriff enters*

**Sheriff**  (*smarmily*) Good-morrow, dear friends.

*The Robbers look around to see if anyone else has walked on behind them,
before they realize he is speaking to them*

  You wouldn't be looking for a job, by any chance?
**Toyle**  (*eagerly*) Not half. We haven't got a penny and we're absolutely
  starving. We came to Nottingham to join Robin Hood's band, but it
  wasn't any use.
**Sheriff**  Why not?
**Trubble**  We couldn't afford the instruments.
**Sheriff**  Then how would you like to work for me? I'll pay you ten pieces
  of gold and all you can eat.
**Robbers**  (*eagerly*) What do we have to do?
**Sheriff**  (*leering at audience*) Just come with me, and I'll explain
  everything.

  *The Sheriff and Robbers exit* R. *As they do so, Marion and the Babes
  enter from* L, *holding hands*

**Marion** That's all very well, but I'm sure poor Nurse Glucose will be worried to death. It was very naughty of you to run away like that.

**Jack** We didn't really run away, Marion. We just wanted to explore the city on our own.

**Jill** We're so tired of being kept inside that horrible old castle all the time.

**Marion** (*sighing*) I know. But England's not the place it used to be. Since King Richard went off to the Crusades, the streets aren't safe. Some people are even too scared to leave their homes at all.

**Jack** But we're only children. No-one would hurt us. (*Anxiously*) Would they?

**Marion** (*quickly*) No, of course not. But just the same ... it might be better if you don't go off exploring on your own again.

**Jill** Do you ever get frightened, Marion?

**Marion** Sometimes. But I never let anyone know about it. You see ... I've got a little secret for making myself seem extra brave. Would you like me to tell you about it?

**Babes** (*eagerly*) Yes, please.

**Marion** Then I will.

### Song 4: Marion and Babes

*They exit at the end of the song*

*The Lights fade quickly to Black-out*

Scene 3

*The old schoolroom. Daytime*

*A classroom. Teacher's desk is UR, angled slightly L, and on it are three white, conical dunce's caps with a large letter D printed on them in red, and a slapstick cane. UC is a blackboard on an easel. A longish nail is embedded in the top L hand corner of the board and painted black so it is invisible to the audience. Chalks and an eraser rest on the easel's ledge. Two long benches are L, one behind the other and angled to face the audience. A shorter bench is in front of these, constructed like a letter "F" face down, so that anyone sitting on the legless end will be tipped on to the floor*

*The classroom is in bedlam. Pupils are racing around or wrestling. Conker fights are taking place and paper darts zoom across the room. Everyone is talking, shouting or laughing and the music plays a spirited version of "Boys and Girls, Come out to Play"*

*Jack and Jill enter* UR *and cross to the benches* L

*Nurse Glucose enters* DR *wearing a cap and gown over her costume and carrying a large handbell. She reacts at the sight in front of her and rings the bell loudly. At once, everyone hurries to their places with much giggling and sits*

**Nurse** (*sternly*) I should think so, too. I've never heard such noise in an academic establishment. Shouting and screaming and running around like lunatics. Where do you think you are? The House of Commons? (*Primly*) Good-morning, children.

**All** (*in unison*) Good-morning, Teacher.

**Nurse** That's better. (*She puts the bell on the desk*) Now then ... I'm Nurse Glucose, your new Headmistress, and the first thing I'm going to do this morning is tell you all about the hippopotamus.

*All pupils begin chattering*

(*Firmly*) No chattering. No chattering. And I want you all to look at me, otherwise you'll never find out what a hippopotamus looks like.

*Pupils all laugh heartily*

*As they do so, Trubble enters* R, *dressed as a little girl*

**Trubble** (*simpering*) Hallo, ev'rybody. (*He waves coyly at the others*)

*All the boys wolf-whistle*

**Nurse** (*glaring at them and then at Trubble*) Never mind "Hallo, ev'rybody". What time do you call this? You're late.

**Trubble** (*simpering*) I know, but I've been writing a beautiful poem.

**Nurse** (*mollified*) Oh. Well. I like a nice poem, meself. But only if it rhymes, though. Does your poem rhyme?

**Trubble** Oh, yes, Miss. Would you like to hear it? (*He strikes a pose and recites*)

> "A pretty young schoolgirl called Nelly,
> Went out for a walk, 'stead of watching the telly.
> She fell in a pond, all gungey and smelly
> And got soaked to the skin, right up to her knees." (*He beams at Nurse*)

*Pupils all applaud loudly*

**Nurse** Just a minute. Just a minute. That last line doesn't rhyme at all.
**Trubble** (*apologetically*) Well ... there wasn't much water in the pond.

*Pupils all laugh*

**Nurse** (*fed up*) Oh, go and sit down.

*Trubble simpers and moves to the empty (short) bench, sitting on the safe end*

Now then ... as I was saying earlier, today I'm going to tell you all about hippopotamusususes, so ——

*Toyle enters* DR *dressed as a schoolboy in short trousers, jacket and cap. He carries a large apple*

**Toyle** Morning, Teacher.
**Nurse** (*reacting*) Where've you popped up from? You should have been here five minutes ago.
**Toyle** (*cheekily*) Why? What happened? (*He chortles*)

*Pupils all laugh*

**Nurse** You're late for school.
**Toyle** Oh, yes. But it wasn't my fault. We've only got back from America this morning.
**Nurse** America?
**Toyle** Yeah. We went to see the Grand Canyon.
**Nurse** (*impressed*) Oh, I say. And did you like it?
**Toyle** Well me and me mum did, but me dad's face dropped a mile.
**Nurse** Why? He wasn't disappointed with the view, was he?
**Toyle** No. He fell over the edge. (*He chortles*)

*Pupils all laugh*

**Nurse** (*grimly*) I see. It's going to be one of those mornings, is it? All right, sunshine. What's your name?
**Toyle** (*blankly*) I don't know, miss.
**Nurse** (*surprised*) You don't know? A big boy like you and you don't know what your name is?

**Toyle**  No, miss.
**Nurse**  Well, what does your mother call you?
**Toyle**  She doesn't call me anything. She likes me.

*Pupils all laugh*

**Nurse**  I think I'll call you Dum-dum. Go and sit down.

*He begins to move away*

  Just a minute. Just a minute. What's that you've got there?
**Toyle**  It's me apple, miss. (*He shows it*) For playtime.
**Nurse**  Yes. Well I'm having no apples rolling around my classroom,
  thank you very much. You can put it somewhere safe for the time being.
**Toyle**  I'll put it on the shelf, then, shall I? (*He moves to the blackboard*)
**Nurse**  (*blankly*) Shelf? Shelf? (*She glances round*) What shelf?
**Toyle**  This one. (*He picks up the chalk, draws a line below the hidden
  nail and pushes the apple on to the nail so it appears to be resting on
  the chalk line*)

*As Nurse gapes, Toyle sits next to Trubble. They grin at each other*

**Nurse**  (*recovering herself*) Well ... It's too late to talk about hippopot-
  amususes now, so we'd better do some arithmetic instead.

*Pupils all groan loudly*

  Now then ... Supposing I had ten apples in this hand ... (*she shows one
  hand*) and seven apples in this hand ... (*she shows the other hand*) what
  would I have?
**Toyle**  Very big hands. (*He chortles*)

*Pupils laugh loudly*

**Nurse**  (*annoyed*) Who said that? Who said that?
**Pupils**  (*with much glee*) Dum-dum.
**Nurse**  (*crossly*) Come out here. (*She gets the cane from the desk*)

*Toyle stands and moves* c

  Turn round and touch your toes.

*He does so and she canes him*

**Toyle** Owwww. (*He jumps up, rubbing his buttocks*)
**Nurse** Now go and sit down.

*He returns to his place and sits as she replaces the cane on the desk and picks up a piece of chalk*

   Right. Now who can tell me what three times three is? (*She writes 3 x 3 on the blackboard*)
**Trubble** (*jumping up*) Me, miss. Me, miss.

*The bench tips and Toyle is pitched on to the floor. Everybody laughs*

**Nurse** (*crossly*) What are you doing down there?
**Toyle** Getting up. (*He struggles to his feet*)
**Nurse** Come out here.

*Protesting, Toyle moves* c *again. Nurse gets the cane as Trubble rights the bench and sits*

   Bend over.

*Still protesting, he bends and she canes him*

**Toyle** (*howling*) Owwww. (*He rubs his buttocks again*)
**Nurse** Now go and sit down and behave yourself. (*She puts the cane back on the desk*)
**Toyle** (*wincing*) I'll behave meself, but I can't sit down. (*He moves back to his seat and sits cautiously*)
**Nurse** Now where was I? (*She remembers*) Oh, yes. Three times three. Any answers?
**Trubble** (*calling*) Please, miss. Eight.
**Nurse** (*pleased*) Clever girl. (*She writes it on the board, then realizes*) What do you mean, "Eight"? Three threes are nine.
**Trubble** Oh, no they're not. And I can prove it.
**Nurse** Oh, can you? All right, little miss smarty-pants. Prove it.

*Trubble stands and Toyle is thrown to the floor again. Pupils laugh. As Nurse glares at Toyle, who hastily rights the bench, turning it the other way round, and sits, Trubble gets the three dunce caps from the desk and returns* c

**Trubble** Three threes are eight. (*He puts the caps in a row in front of him*) One. (*He picks up a cap*) Two. (*He picks up another cap*) Three. (*He indicates the third one*) Four. (*He puts one cap down*) Five. (*He puts the other cap down*) Six. (*He picks up a cap*) Seven. (*He picks up another*) Eight. (*He picks up the final cap*) See? Three threes are eight. (*He gives a small curtsy*)

*Pupils all applaud*

**Nurse** No, no, no, no, no, no, no. That's not right. It's all wrong. (*To the audience*) Isn't it, girls and boys?
**Toyle** (*standing*) Course it's wrong. Three threes are eleven.
**Nurse** (*thankfully*) Of course they are. (*She realizes*) What are you talking about? How can three threes be eleven?
**Toyle** I'll show you. (*He pushes Trubble aside and takes the caps*)

*Trubble sits c of the bench*

One. (*He puts a cap on the floor*) Two. (*He puts the second one down*) Three. (*He holds it up to show them, then picks up the other two as he speaks*) Four. Five. (*He puts one cap down*) Six. (*He puts another down*) Seven. (*He puts the last one down*) Eight. (*He picks them up again rapidly*) Nine. Ten. Eleven.

*NB The faster this gag is worked, the better*

*Pupils all cheer, whistle, shout, etc., while Nurse is completely baffled*

**Nurse** (*spluttering*) Go and sit down. (*She snatches the caps from him and takes them back to the desk*)

*Toyle returns to the bench and sits, forcing Trubble to shuffle up on to the unsafe end. Toyle closes his eyes*

It's quite oblivious that none of you know anything at all about mathematics, so we'd better start right at the beginning. (*She points at Trubble*) You. Come out here.

*Trubble stands and moves c*

Right. Now let's see how far you can count.
**Trubble** One, two, three, four, five, six, seven, eight, nine, ten.

**Nurse**  Well, go on. What comes after ten?
**Trubble**  Jack, Queen, King.

*Pupils all laugh*

  (*Tiredly*) I think we'll forget mathematics. Go and sit down.

*Trubble goes back to the bench and sits*

  We'll try a bit of History instead.

*All groan loudly*

  First question coming up ...

*Toyle lets out a loud snore and Pupils all laugh*

  (*Grimly*) I say. Rip van Winkle.

*He snores again*

  (*Louder*) I say.

*Trubble nudges him, but Toyle carries on snoring. Nurse crosses to him and bellows in his ear*

  I say.

*Toyle jerks awake with a start*

  What do you think you're doing ? You can't go to sleep here.
**Toyle**  (*indignantly*) I could if you stopped shouting.

*Pupils all laugh*

**Nurse**  (*spluttering*) Yes. Well, pay a little attention. (*She moves back* C)
**Toyle**  (*muttering*) I'm paying as little as I can.
**Nurse**  Now then (*not looking at him*) who was the son of the Black
  Prince?
**Trubble**  (*loudly*) Old King Cole.

*Pupils all laugh*

**Nurse** (*turning round*) Who said that?
**Pupils** (*gleefully*) Dum-dum.
**Nurse** Come out here. Come out here. (*She gets the cane again*)

*Toyle and Trubble rise together and as Toyle, protesting loudly, moves*
*c and bends over, Trubble reverses the bench once more*

(*Rolling her sleeves up, grimly*) Right. This time you're really for it.
(*She raises the cane*)
**Trubble** Just a minute. Just a minute.
**Nurse** What for ?
**Trubble** (*bursting into tears*) It wasn't him that said it at all. It was me.
And I can't let you cane him for something I did. (*He hurries forward*
*and bends over behind Toyle, his hands resting on Toyle's hips*) Cane
me, instead.
**Nurse** Don't you worry. I certainly will. One ... Two … Three.

*As she says "three", Trubble springs on to Toyle's back so that Toyle*
*receives the blow intended for Trubble. He howls and the Pupils all laugh*
*loudly. Trubble slides down again*

(*Not having noticed*) Right. Go and sit down. The pair of you.

*They return to the bench and sit*

(*Replacing the cane*) Now let's get on with the lesson.
**Trubble** (*standing*) Please, Miss.
**Nurse** What is it now?
**Trubble** Can I ask you a question?
**Nurse** (*undecided*) Oh, I suppose so. What is it?
**Trubble** What's the difference between a buffalo and a bison?
**Nurse** (*baffled*) A buffalo and a bison? I don't know. What is the
difference?
**Trubble** You can't wash your hands in a buffalo. (*He sits down*)

*Pupils all giggle and laugh*

**Nurse** (*grimly*) Right. That's done it. That's *done* it. One more sound
from anybody, and I'll send you all home.

*At once, everybody begins to talk, shout, whistle, etc.*

*The Sheriff enters* DR. *At once the noise subsides*

**Sheriff** (*loudly*) And what's going on here, might I ask? I could hear this disgraceful revelry in (*local street*).

**Nurse** (*defensively*) Well it's no use looking at me. They're all young hooligans. They're worse than French Farmers.

**Sheriff** Nonsense, madam. You are an incompetent teacher.

**Nurse** (*indignantly*) I beg your puddin'. I'm nothing of the suchwich. I've been certified, I have. By the Ministry of Exclamation.

**Toyle** Rubbish. She can't even teach sums right.

**Sheriff** Indeed? (*To Nurse*) Then in that case, I'll have to give you the sack and you won't get paid a penny.

**Nurse** Ooo-er. (*Quickly*) Just a minute. Just a minute. I'll show you whether I can teach sums or not. Sit down over there. (*She indicates the small bench*)

*The Sheriff crosses to it pompously and sits on the unsafe end*

Now then ... Jack and Jill ... What are seven thirteens?

**Babes** (*standing*) Twenty-eight, Miss.

*Everyone sniggers*

**Nurse** Quite right. See? (*She pokes her tongue out at the Sheriff*)

*Jack and Jill sit again*

**Sheriff** (*standing*) What do you mean "Quite right"? Seven thirteens aren't twenty-eight.

**Nurse** Oh, yes they are.

**Pupils** Oh, no they're not.

**Nurse** Oh, yes they are — and I'll prove it.

*The Sheriff sits again and Nurse gets the eraser and cleans the blackboard before picking up the chalk*

Right. (*She writes 13 on the blackboard and writes a 7 below the 3*) Seven threes are twenty-one. (*She writes a 2 down*) That's two down and one to carry. And seven ones are seven ... plus the one left over makes eight. (*She writes 8 after the 2*) So thirteen sevens make twenty-eight.

*Pupils all laugh and applaud*

**Sheriff** (*standing again*) But that's wrong, you stupid old faggot. All
wrong. Divide twenty-eight by seven and you'll see it is. (*He sits again*)
**Nurse** All right. (*She cleans the board*) We'll divide it, then. (*She writes
28 on the board, then a division line, finally placing the 7 in position*)
Seven into two won't go, so we'll put the two over here. (*She writes a
2 on the far edge of the board*) And seven into eight goes once ... (*she
writes a 1 on top of the division line*) with one left over. And one and
these two here (*she indicates the 2*), makes three. (*She writes 3 down
after the 1*) So seven into twenty-eight is thirteen. Simple.

*Pupils all applaud and cheer again*

**Sheriff** (*standing in annoyance*) This is ridiculous. Write thirteen down
seven times, one under the other, and add them up. You can't possibly
get twenty-eight that way. (*He sits again*)
**Nurse** All right. We'll add them up. (*She cleans the board and writes 13
down seven times, one below the other*) And just to show there's no
cheating, everybody can help me count them up. All together now ...
(*she counts the 3's*) Three, six, nine, twelve, fifteen, eighteen, twenty-
one, (*she counts the 1's*) twenty-two, twenty-three, twenty-four,
twenty-five, twenty-six, twenty-seven, twenty-eight. (*She throws the
chalk into the air in triumph*)

*The classroom explodes in a riot of cheers. Toyle and Trubble jump to
their feet and the Sheriff is pitched to the floor. Pupils pelt him with paper
balls, etc., and the scene ends in total chaos*

SCENE 4

*A path in Sherwood Forest. Evening*

*Marion enters L, wearing a cloak over her gown and carrying a lantern*

**Marion** (*calling softly*) Robin? (*She glances around*) Robin?

*Friar Tuck enters R. He is a portly, jovial man in a friar's robe, and he
too carries a lantern*

**Friar** Who's there? (*He raises his lantern*)
**Marion** (*relieved*) Friar Tuck.
**Friar** That's odd. I could have sworn I was over here. (*He laughs*

*heartily*) Lady Marion. Welcome to Sherwood Forest again. (*He moves towards her*)

**Marion** Thank you, good Father. But I'm looking for Robin. I've just got to speak to him. Is he around?

**Friar** Ay. But he's just about to leave for London with Little John. (*He lowers his voice*) There's a rumour King Richard's returning to England, and they want to find out how true it is.

**Marion** (*fervently*) Oh, if only it is. But I *must* see him before he leaves.

**Friar** He'll be here in the twinkling of an eye. (*He turns and waves his lantern to someone off* R)

**Marion** I hope I'm not being silly, but there's something strange going on at the castle and I'm rather worried.

*Robin enters* R. *His bow is in his hand and a quiver of arrows on his back*

**Robin** (*delightedly*) Marion. What are you doing here? (*He crosses to her*)

**Marion** (*anxiously*) Oh, Robin. It's the Babes. I'm sure they're in some sort of danger. I've seen the way Uncle Cedric keeps looking at them ... and those two villains who tried to rob me a few weeks ago are following them all over Nottingham. Even into school.

**Robin** (*frowning*) Are you sure?

*Marion gives a worried nod*

(*Reassuringly*) It's probably nothing to worry about. I mean ... who'd harm two innocent children? But all the same, I'll have some of my men keep an eye on them, too. (*To Friar Tuck*) Tuck. Get Will Scarlett, Alan a-Dale and some of the others.

*Friar Tuck exits* R

Don't worry, Marion. If there is some nasty little plan brewing in the Sheriff's head, we'll soon put a stop to it.

**Marion** (*relieved*) Thank you. I couldn't bear it if anything happened to them. (*She changes the subject*) Friar Tuck tells me you're going to London.

**Robin** Yes. But I'll be back for the Goose Fair next week. I hear Prince John's given a golden arrow as a prize for the best archer ... and I mean to claim it for myself.

**Marion** (*shocked*) But you mustn't come to the Fair, Robin. It'll be crawling with Uncle Cedric's men.

**Robin** (*amused*) So what? I'll be there with my own band of Merry Men.

*Friar Tuck, Will Scarlett, Alan a-Dale, Much the Miller's son, Little John, etc. enter. A few ladies may also be included if space permits*

And I'd like to see the soldiers who'd stand up to them.

**Marion** (*smiling*) You're right. But promise you'll be careful, just the same.

**Will** Don't worry, Lady Marion. We'll take care of him.

**Much** And the Sheriff's men as well.

*All laugh heartily*

**Robin** (*to Marion*) Now you'd better get back to the castle before the Sheriff finds out you're missing. I'll make sure the Babes are protected and I'll see you the minute I return from London.

**Marion** Oh, I wish I were going with you. I've never been there. What's it like, Robin?

**Robin** London? Well ... it's like ... like ... I can't explain it. It's just London.

### Song 5: Robin and Company

*At the end of the song all exit* L. *The Fairy enters from* R *in a white follow spot*

**Fairy** Brave Robin Hood your part you'll play
In putting wrongs to right,
But wicked Sheriff Spindleshanks
Has made his plans to strike tonight.
He fancies that the coast is clear,
That the Babes lie unprotected,
And through a secret passageway
Has brought his henchmen undetected.
So whilst within those ancient walls
Both Nurse and Babes prepare for sleep,
With all due speed I'll hasten there
My vigil through the night to keep.

*Black-out*

SCENE 5

*The Babes' bedroom. Evening*

*A large bed is* UC, *with a small bedside table next to it. A rocking chair is* DL *with a thick fairy story book on it*

*Jack and Jill, both in their nightclothes, are playing with their toys. Nurse Glucose enters* UL

**Nurse** (*surprised*) Aren't you in bed yet? It's nearly ten o'clock. When I was your age, if I wasn't in bed by ten, I went home. (*She realizes what she has said*) I mean ... hurry up. Or there'll be no time for a story.

*They reluctantly leave their toys and turn towards the bed*

Just a minute. Have you cleaned your teeth?

*They turn back and shake their heads guiltily*

I thought not. It's very important to clean your teeth. (*To the audience*) Isn't it, girls and boys?

*Audience reaction*

(*To the Babes*) You see? (*To the audience*) Show the children how nice and clean your teeth look when you've had them brushed. Go on. Show 'em your teeth. (*She reels back*) I said show 'em, love. Not take 'em out. (*She winces*) Oh, no. She's passing 'em round, now. (*To the Babes*) Off you go. Quickly. And use plenty of toothpaste.

*The Babes exit* UR

Oh ... I wonder if that milk's boiling yet? I'd better go see.

*She exits* UL. *As she does so, the Sheriff creeps in* DR *and heads* C, *followed by Toyle and Trubble, who are now in their normal clothes*

**Sheriff** (*over his shoulder*) Shhhhhhhh.
**Toyle** (*over his shoulder*) Shhhhhhhh.
**Trubble** (*over his shoulder*) Shhhhhhhh. (*He realizes there is no-one else there*)

**Sheriff** (*in a whisper*) Here we are. The Babes' bedroom.

**Toyle** (*glancing around*) It's a bit creepy, isn't it?

**Sheriff** (*snarling*) Of course it's a bit creepy, you nematoidical nerd. That's why I put them in here. There's an old legend about this room ... An old legend that anyone who enters here goes stark staring mad. (*He laughs wildly*)

**Trubble** Blimey. Sounds just like the Planning Department of (*local District Council*).

**Sheriff** (*pulling himself together*) Now then. You know exactly what it is you have to do?

**Toyle** (*nodding*) We grab the kids ... take 'em deep into the forest, then leave 'em all alone.

**Sheriff** (*eagerly*) That's it. That's it. Absolutely perfect.

**Trubble** And to get this Duke of Edinburgh's Award, they've got to find their own way back here? Right?

**Sheriff** Precisely.

**Trubble** Seems daft to me. There's all sorts of wild animals in that forest. Two little children could get eaten alive.

**Sheriff** (*beaming*) Yes. (*He recovers quickly*) Oh, they'll be perfectly safe, I assure you. They've practised it dozens of times.

**Toyle** (*disappointedly*) Pity it isn't something more horrible you want us to do. After all, we're professional villains, you know. Not Boy Scouts.

**Sheriff** (*interested*) Well ... there *is* something else you could do for me, if you're willing?

**Trubble** What's that?

**Sheriff** (*putting his arm round Trubble's shoulder*) How would you like to earn *another* ten pieces of gold ... for doing something very naughty indeed?

**Trubble** (*jumping away quickly and glowering at Sheriff*) Gerroff.

**Sheriff** (*hastily*) No, no. You misunderstand me. What I meant was ... just to make it a bit more difficult for them to find their way back again ... perhaps you could ... er ... slit their throats or something?

*The Robbers look at each other*

**Toyle** (*suspiciously*) You mean ... you want us to murder 'em?

**Sheriff** (*anguished*) Shhhhhhhh. (*He glances round quickly*) Of course I don't want you to murder them. Certainly not. Whatever gave you that idea? I wouldn't harm a hair of their sweet little heads.

**Toyle** (*disappointed*) Shame about that. We could have used another ten pieces of gold.

**Sheriff** (*delightedly*) You mean — you'll do it? (*Relieved*) Splendid. Then meet me in the market-place tomorrow morning and I'll see you get everything you deserve. (*Aside*) A quick hanging, together with that cursed Robin Hood. (*Aloud*) Till tomorrow, then.

*He exits* DL

**Trubble** (*to Toyle*) Here ... what did you mean by telling him we'd murder 'em? I'm killing no children.

**Toyle** (*patiently*) Course we're not going to kill 'em, stupid. But if he thinks we have done, we get ten more pieces of gold, don't we?

**Trubble** (*the light dawning*) Oh, I never thought of that.

**Toyle** No. You never do think, do you? Now let's find somewhere to hide so we can grab the Babes as soon as they come to bed.

**Nurse** (*off*) I'm coming back, children.

*The Robbers panic*

**Toyle** Quick. Into the bed.

*They dive into the bed and pull the sheets up over their heads*

*Nurse enters* UL *carrying a large bottle of castor oil and a ladle*

**Nurse** (*brightly*) Here we are. Some nice castor oil before you have your cocoa. (*She moves to the bed*) And it's no use hiding under the sheets. They haven't invented All-Bran yet, so you need a good dose of this. (*She pours out a ladle of liquid, then puts the bottle on the table*) One for you, dear.

*She pokes Toyle in the stomach with her free hand. He sits up with a gasp. She pulls the sheet away without looking and tips the ladle towards his open mouth. He swallows the liquid*

**Toyle** (*anguished*) Aaaaaaaaagh. (*He throws himself back and covers himself with the sheet again, twitching, writhing and moaning*)

*Nurse picks up the bottle, pours out another ladleful, puts the bottle back on the table and moves round the bed to the* R *side*

**Nurse** And one for you.

*The business is repeated as before*

**Trubble** Gaaaaaaaaaaaar. (*He drops back and covers himself up again, moaning*)

**Nurse** (*primly*) Such a fuss over a little drop of castor oil. (*She moves back to the table and picks up the bottle to exit*)

*Jack and Jill enter behind her*

Anybody would think it tasted horrible. (*She still doesn't notice them*) Why, when *I* was a little girl I thought nothing of drinking two bottles of castor oil a *day*. It was lovely.

*The Babes exchange glances*

**Jack** I bet you wouldn't drink it now.

**Nurse** (*turning to them*) Who wouldn't? (*She blinks*) What are you doing out of bed again? Never mind. Just stay there and I'll show you. (*She pours out a ladleful*) Through the mouth and past the gums, look out stomach, here it comes. (*She drinks the liquid*) See? (*She puts the bottle and spoon down on the table*) Delicious. (*She reacts*) Aaaaaaaaaagh.

*She dances round spluttering and choking as the Babes laugh*

*Toyle and Trubble quickly slide out of the bed and exit* UR *without being seen*

(*Recovering*) Oh ... my whole life flashed before me. I was up to fifty-seven — I mean twenty-six — before I stopped counting. (*She pats her throat*) Now quickly, children. Into bed again.

**Jill** Tell us a story, Nurse Glucose.

**Nurse** Certainly not. It's too late.

**Jack** But we're not tired.

**Nurse** No. But I am. Now get into bed.

**Jill** Oh, please, Nurse Glucose. You're the best story-teller in the whole wide world.

**Nurse** (*relenting*) Oh, you certainly know how to get round your old Nursie, don't you? Go on. Say your prayers and get into bed and I'll see what I can do.

*The Babes kneel at the side of the bed to say their prayers as Nurse sits in the rocking chair and looks through the book of fairy stories*

(*Glancing at them*) Are you saying those prayers, children?

**Babes** Yes, Nurse.
**Nurse** I can't hear them.
**Jack** But we're not saying them to you.
**Nurse** (*she reacts; then*) No. (*She quickly looks back at the book*)

*The Babes scramble into bed and cover themselves*

**Jill** Nurse?
**Nurse** (*still occupied*) Yes, dear?
**Jill** You won't ever go away and leave us, will you?
**Nurse** (*startled*) Of course not, dear. Whatever gave you that idea?
**Jack** Uncle Cedric told the Captain of the Guard that as soon as he'd got
  rid of his unwanted encumbrances, he'd be getting rid of you, too.
  (*Puzzled*) What's an unwanted encumbrance, Nurse?
**Nurse** Oh, I think it's just some kind of rheumatism, dear. There's a lot
  of it about in draughty old places like this. Now don't you worry your
  heads. Nursie's going nowhere. Not without you two. After all ...
  you're all I've got left in the world now.

### Song 6: Nurse

*By the end of the song, the Babes are asleep and Nurse, too, is feeling
sleepy*

Oh, dear. (*She yawns*) I feel ever so sleepy myself. I think I'll just
snuggle down here for a few minutes and have a little snooze. Perhaps
I'll dream about meeting a handsome fairy prince? Mind you ... (*she
yawns*) If he's a fairy I don't expect there'll be much doing. (*She closes
her eyes and falls asleep*)

*The Lights dim*

*The Fairy enters* DR *in a spotlight*

**Fairy** In silence now the castle sleeps.
  Through windows tall, the pale moon peeps.
  And as the Robbers foul have fled,
  The Babes rest safely in their bed.
  So come, sweet dreams, 'tis time for play,
  The hours of night to while away.

*She waves her wand and Toys emerge from cupboards and wings to
join her in a dream ballet*

## Ballet of Toys and Fairy

*At the end of the ballet, Toys and Fairy exit*

*Jack sits up sleepily and looks around*

**Jack**  Nurse Glucose?

*Nurse snores gently. Jack slides out of bed and begins to exit* UL. *Jill wakes and sits up*

**Jill**  (*sleepily*) Where are you going?
**Jack**  (*tiredly*) I want a drink of water and Nursie's asleep.
**Jill**  (*sleepily*) Can I have one, too?
**Jack**  (*yawning*) Come on, then.

*He exits* UL. *Jill gets up and follows him off*

*Nurse snuffles in her sleep and twitches*

**Nurse**  Ohhhh. Ohhhhhhhh. (*She suddenly sits up, her eyes still closed*) I'm so tired. I'll just finish me cocoa then I'm off to bed. (*She mimes drinking from a cup, then rises and totters* UL, *her fingers still gripping the imaginary cup. Suddenly she stops dead. Tiredly*) I'll wash this in the morning. (*She tosses the invisible cup aside and continues towards the bed*)

*There is the sound of a breaking cup off* L. *She stops dead in her tracks again, shrugs, then continues to bed and climbs in*

Nighty-night, dears. Nighty-night. (*She pulls the covers over her*)

*The Lights dim further*

*Toyle and Trubble enter from opposite sides, back to back. With great caution they move towards* C *and collide. With yells of fear they turn and see each other*

**Toyle** }
**Trubble** }  (*together*) Shhhhhhhhhhhh.
**Toyle**  Quick. Now's our chance. The old faggot must have gone to bed. Let's grab the Babes.

*They hurry to the bed and grab the sleeping figure, sheets and all. Nurse awakes and begins to yell and struggle*

*The Robbers hurry her off R in triumph. As they do so, the Babes enter from L and watch in dismay*

*Black-out*

CURTAIN

# ACT II

*Nottingham Goose Fair. Daytime*

*An old English fairground, with backdrop of gaily striped tents and stalls, backed by Sherwood Forest*

*When the* Curtain *opens, the Citizens of Nottingham, led by Maid Marion, are singing and dancing as the business of the Fair flows on around them*

### Song 7: Marion and Citizens

*After the song all fall back, laughing, leaving Marion* c

**Marion** (*happily*) Oh, what fun we're having here at the Goose Fair. I can't remember when I've enjoyed myself so much. (*Longingly*) If only Robin were here, everything would be perfect.

*The Sheriff enters* UL

**Sheriff** (*to the Citizens in his path*) Out of my way, peasants. (*He pushes through*) Marion, my dear. (*He moves down to her*) So there you are. I was wondering where you'd got to. (*He leers at her*)
**Marion** (*frostily*) I was enjoying myself with friends, Uncle Cedric.
**Sheriff** (*mock hurt*) And aren't I your friend, my dear?
**Marion** I don't think so, Uncle Cedric.
**Sheriff** (*smarmily*) Oh, come now. Surely you're not still upset about that silly little incident last week? (*He laughs dismissively*)
**Marion** (*hotly*) It wasn't a silly little incident at all. Poor Nurse Glucose. Dragged out of bed by two horrible villains in the middle of the night. She must have had a terrible shock. Thank goodness the night watchman saw them in time and frightened them off.
**Sheriff** (*easily*) How very true. But I still don't see why you should think it had anything to do with *me*? Why ... I hardly knew the men.
**Marion** You knew them well enough to have them follow Jack and Jill all over Nottingham.

**Sheriff** Well ... er ... that was for the children's own protection. After all ... with fifty thousand pounds in their possession, who knows what villains might be trying to get their hands on it. If Robin Hood knew about it, for instance ... (*he shrugs expressively*)

**Marion** Robin would never steal from children. And besides ... he's got his own men keeping an eye on them.

**Sheriff** (*shaken*) What?

**Marion** That's right. If anyone goes near them, they'll have to answer to the Merry Men.

**Sheriff** (*aside*) Curses. (*Aloud*) Well ... I'm very glad to hear it, my dear. But come. It's almost time for the jousting contest. We should be taking our places in my private viewing box. (*He offers his arm*)

**Marion** (*ignoring it*) If you don't mind, I'd rather walk there with my friends. (*To the Citizens*) Come along, everyone.

*Marion and Citizens exit* UL

**Sheriff** (*annoyed*) Blast that interfering outlaw. How dare he meddle in my machinations? (*He looks around*) Where are those neanderthalic nincompoops, Toyle and Trubble? I must find them at once and warn them.

*He exits* DR *in haste. Nurse Glucose enters* UL *in a dress with a huge bustle*

**Nurse** Oh, girls and boys. I'm just on the way to collect Jack and Jill from the roundabouts, but I must tell you ... You wouldn't believe the week I've had. First of all, two horrible men tried to kidnap me, then the next day I nearly got landed with someone else's Council Tax. I did. The postman said, "Here, missis, is this letter for you? The name's illegible." I said, "Certainly not. My name's Glucose." (*She beams*) Mind you ... he was a bit of all right. The postman. I was doing some baking when he arrived and he could hardly wait to get his hands on me "Fancies". (*She hoists her bosom*) Saucy young devil. Oh, but what a sun-tan he had. I said, "Here", I said, "have you been on holiday, then?", and he said, "Yes. I've just got back from Blackpool." Well, I love Blackpool, don't you, girls and boys? So I said "Fancy that. And did you go on a donkey?" He said "No. I went on a train from (*local railway station*)." (*She sighs*) Oh, but I can't remember the last time *I* went on holiday. And I could really do with a bit of sunshine after living in Nottingham Castle. Talk about draughty. I think they must have built the place with breezeblocks. I mean ... even in summer you get cold feet. I complained to the Sheriff about it last week. I said, " My feet haven't been warm since the day we arrived here," and all he said was, "Well, use a hot water bottle, then." (*Scornfully*) Use a hot water bottle. He must think I'm an idiot or something. I tried a hot water bottle the first night we got here, and it wasn't the slightest bit of use. I mean, you can't get your feet through that stupid little hole in the neck, can you?

*Jack and Jill enter* UR

(*Seeing them*) Oh, there you are. I was just coming to look for you. Did you enjoy yourselves?

**Jill**  Oh, yes. It was ever so exciting.

**Jack**  What shall we do next?

**Nurse**  Well, we could go and watch the parade.

**Jill**  (*delightedly*) A parade?

**Jack**  (*excitedly*) With trumpets and things?

**Nurse**  That's right, dears. Trumpets, drums, bassoons ... in fact, the biggest parade you've ever seen in your life ... and it's just about to start.

### Song 8: Nurse and Babes

*As they sing, the Citizens enter and join in. At the end of the song, all exit* R *in triumph. A moment later, Toyle and Trubble hurry on from* UL *and move* DC

**Toyle**  This way. They came this way. (*He looks around*) Oh, no. Where've they got to now?

**Trubble**  (*worried*) Oh, I don't like this, Toyle. We shouldn't be here at the Goose Fair. Not since last week. Every policeman in Nottingham's looking for us.

**Toyle**  I know. I know. But if we don't grab the Babes and take 'em into Sherwood Forest, we're never going to get that gold we were promised.

**Trubble**  Couldn't we just rob the public instead?

**Toyle**  Too late. The Government's doing that already.

**Trubble**  Well, why don't we open a stall in the Fair and sell Truth Drug?

**Toyle**  Truth Drug?

**Trubble**  (*producing a small bottle from his pocket*) Yes. I invented it last night. One sip of this and you've got to tell the truth.

**Toyle**  (*scornfully*) Give over.

**Trubble**  It's true. And it works on anybody but a politician.

**Toyle**  (*curious*) Why won't it work on a politician?

**Trubble**  Because nothing'll make them tell the truth.

**Toyle**  (*snatching the bottle*) Here. Let me taste that. (*He takes a drink then spits it out in disgust*) Aghhhhhhhh! That's diesel oil.

**Trubble**  (*taking the bottle back*) That's the truth. (*He laughs*)

**Toyle**  (*annoyed*) Oooh, you're as thick as two short planks, you are. (*Loudly*) Owwwwwww. (*He clutches at his cheek*) That's started my tooth aching now. (*He moans*) I'll have to go to the dentist.

**Trubble**  Don't be daft. You don't need a dentist when your tooth aches. Whenever *I* get a toothache, I go round to my girlfriend's house and she kisses me, and cuddles me, and caresses me ... and after a few minutes, the pain's gone. Just like that. (*He snaps his fingers*) So why don't you do what I do?

**Toyle**  Well, it's worth a try, I suppose. Where does your girlfriend live?

*There is the sound of a fanfare*

(*Glancing off* L) Look out. Somebody's coming. Hide.

*The Robbers scuttle off* DR *as the Citizens begin to enter* R *and* L, *followed by the Sheriff, Marion and the Bailiff, who carries a golden arrow on a velvet cushion. The Sheriff and Marion move* UC, *and the Bailiff stands to one side of them*

**Sheriff**  (*grandly*) And now, Citizens of Nottingham ... the Grand Archery Competition.

*All cheer loudly*

And this year's prize is a golden arrow ...

*The Bailiff displays the arrow*

... presented by His Royal Highness, Prince John. Hip, hip ...

*The Citizens are silent*

(*Disconcerted*) Yes. (*Loudly*) Let the contestants stand forth.

*Will Scarlett and Much, the Miller's son, enter. Each carries a bow and arrows*

*The Citizens applaud*

(*Glaring at them*) Is this all? A pathetic pair. Bah. They couldn't hit a barn door if they were standing next to it. (*Grandly*) Out of the way. I'll show them what a real archer can do. (*He snatches Will's bow and arrow, stands facing off* L, *and notches the arrow. Smugly*) Watch this. (*He releases the arrow which shoots off into the wings, then turns to the crowd, smirking*)

*There is a loud yell of pain off* L *and all react*

*Nurse hurries on from* L, *followed by Jack and Jill*

**Nurse** Here. Did you see where that arrow landed?
**Sheriff** (*airily*) No. Tell me.
**Nurse** (*indignantly*) I'll do better than that. I'll show you. (*She turns round to reveal the arrow embedded in her bustle*)

*All react. The Sheriff quickly hands the bow back to Will*

**Sheriff** (*hastily*) Let the first contestant fire.

*Much steps forward, notches his arrow and fires off* L. *All watch with interest, then cheer loudly*

(*Sniffing*) Not bad. Not bad. But you missed the bull's-eye. Next.

*Will tries next. Again, all watch with interest, then cheer loudly*

Slightly better, I suppose. But not good enough. (*He smirks*) Oh, well. It looks like I'd better keep the golden arrow myself.

*He takes the arrow from the cushion as everyone jeers*

Silence, you insolent dogs. The prize is mine.

*Robin Hood enters from* DR *with his bow and arrows. He is disguised in a hooded cloak that hides his face from the Sheriff*

**Robin** One moment, my Lord Sheriff. There is one more contestant.

*All turn to look at him*

**Sheriff** (*sneering*) Go away, old man. You couldn't even bend a bow ... never mind fire an arrow.

**Citizens** (*variously*) Give him a chance. Shame! Coward! Cheat!, *etc.*
**Sheriff** (*stung*) Very well. Fire away. (*Scornfully*) Grandfather.

*Robin notches his arrow, aims* L, *and fires. All watch, then cheer loudly*

**Marion** (*delightedly*) Bull's-eye! The old man wins.
**Sheriff** (*balefully*) Bah. (*To Robin*) Here, you flea-bitten old tramp. Take
it. (*He holds out the arrow to Robin*)

*Robin hands his bow to Will and takes the arrow*

**Robin** I thank you. (*He moves* DR)

*All congratulate him*

**Sheriff** Just a minute. Just a minute. I suppose I'd better have your name.
**Robin** With pleasure, my lord. (*He flings off his cloak*) It's Robin Hood.

*All react*

**Marion** (*delightedly*) Robin.
**Sheriff** (*loudly*) Guards. Guards. Arrest that man.

*There is great confusion, with people shouting and scattering in all
directions*

**Marion** (*calling*) Run, Robin. Run!

*Laughing, Robin waves to her then dashes off* R, *followed by everyone but
the Babes, who stay where they are*

**Jack** (*jumping up and down*) He's getting away. He's getting away!
**Jill** (*excitedly*) Hooray!

*They dance around happily*

   *Toyle and Trubble enter and see them*

**Toyle** Quick. Now's our chance.

*They dash over and grab the Babes*

**Babes** (*shouting*) Help. Help. Let go. Get off me, *etc.*

**Trubble** To the forest with them.

*They carry the screaming and struggling Babes off* L. *As they do so, Nurse enters from* R *and sees them*

**Nurse** (*in a panic*) The children. The children. They've kidnapped the children. Help. Help! (*She dashes around in alarm*)

*The Lights fade rapidly to Black-out*

SCENE 2

*A quiet street. Daytime*

*Toyle and Trubble hurry on from* L, *still carrying the struggling Babes, then exit* R

*The Citizens hurry on from* L *in hot pursuit. With loud calls, they exit* R

*The Sheriff enters from* L

**Sheriff** Bah. That confounded outlaw Robin Hood escaped again. (*He smirks*) But thanks to him and the confusion he caused ... my two helpers managed to kidnap those nauseous Babes at last. An hour from now, they'll both be dead and their fifty thousand pounds will be mine. All mine. (*He laughs nastily*)

*Nurse Glucose enters from* L, *clutching a handkerchief and looking miserable*

**Nurse** (*unhappily*) Oh, girls and boys. Whatever are we going to do? Poor Jack and Jill. Carried off by two horrible kidnappers. Talk about history repeating itself. (*She sniffles into her handkerchief*)
**Sheriff** (*surprised*) You mean they've been kidnapped before?
**Nurse** No. But I have. I was carried off by a gang of crackpots who threatened to cut out my tongue and boil me alive if your brother didn't send them a million pounds in ransom money.
**Sheriff** (*amazed*) What? And he paid it?
**Nurse** Course he didn't. He wasn't that rich.
**Sheriff** Then how come you're still alive?
**Nurse** They sent me home with the ransom note. (*As the thought strikes her*) Here ... I wonder if there'll be a ransom for the Babes?

**Sheriff** Ransom? (*Scornfully*) If you ask me, they're probably lying in Sherwood Forest with their throats cut ...

*Nurse reacts in horror*

... poor little mites. (*He turns his head away and gloats nastily*)
**Nurse** (*faintly*) Oh, I feel all of a tiz-was.
**Sheriff** (*in mock sorrow*) I also. Who'd have thought it would end like this? (*Bravely*) But don't worry, Nurse Glucose. They may be dead, but their money's safe with me. I'll look after it. (*He attempts to look noble*)
**Nurse** (*tearfully*) Oh, thank you. (*She dabs at her eyes, then looks puzzled*) What money?
**Sheriff** Why ... their fifty thousand pounds, of course. As their only living relative, naturally it will all come to me.
**Nurse** (*shaking her head*) Oh, no, dear. Your poor brother took care of that in his will. If anything happened to the children, it was all left to me.
**Sheriff** (*startled*) What?
**Nurse** Every single penny. (*Her eyes watering again*) But I don't want it. I just want the Babes back. (*She sniffles tearfully*)
**Sheriff** (*aside*) Curses. Foiled again. The only way I'm going to get hold of that gold now is to marry the old faggot. (*As the thought strikes him*) And I'd better propose to her now before some other idiot does it. (*To her. Sweetly*) Eczema, my dear ... (*he takes hold of her hand*)
**Nurse** (*startled*) Eh?
**Sheriff** (*fervently*) I can't bear to see you upset like this. You may have lost the Babes, but perhaps *I* can comfort you in your hour of sorrow? How would you like to marry me? (*He smiles at her*)
**Nurse** (*to audience*) Look at those teeth. They're so yellow, every time he smiles, the traffic slows down to see whether it should stop or go. (*To Sheriff*) Marry you?
**Sheriff** (*passionately*) Yes, yes.
**Nurse** And be a Sheriffess?
**Sheriff** (*ardently*) Of course.
**Nurse** (*doubtfully*) Oh, I don't know. I'll have to think about it.
**Sheriff** (*pressing the point*) You can't grieve forever, you know.
**Nurse** (*weakening*) Yes, you're right. And I'm not getting any younger, am I? In another ten years, I'll be almost thirty. (*She decides*) Oh, all right then. I'll marry you on one condition.
**Sheriff** (*warily*) What's that?
**Nurse** That when we get the Babes back, you'll look after them as though they were your own dear children.

**Sheriff** (*expansively*) But, of course, my angel. My very intention. (*He turns his head away and smiles in triumph*)

**Nurse** Oh, and there's just one other thing. I know it sounds silly ... but a young girl like me does need her reassurances. (*She simpers*) Tell me ...Will you still love me when I'm old and ugly?

**Sheriff** (*passionately*) My angel ... you may grow older, but in my eyes, you could never grow uglier.

**Nurse** (*flattered*) Oh, you saucy old thing.

### Song 9: Sheriff and Nurse

*At the end of the song, the Sheriff triumphantly escorts Nurse off* L

*The Lights fade as they exit*

*The Fairy enters* R *in a white follow spot*

**Fairy**   Though it may seem the Sheriff's scheme
Is destined to succeed,
Brave Robin Hood shall foil his plan
And punish him for knavish deed.
So for amusement, come with me
And watch the Sheriff's fall.
This tale will end in merriment
And happiness for almost all.
(*Brightly*) To Sherwood Forest, then, where in
A secret, leafy, glade,
The outlaw band rejoices,
Each Merry Man and his maid.

*She waves her wand and exits* R

*Black-out*

### Scene 3

*A clearing in Sherwood Forest. Early evening*

*The Merry Men and a scattering of Citizens are enjoying themselves*

### Song 10: Company

*At the end of the song, Friar Tuck steps forward*

**Friar**  Greetings, dear friends from Nottingham. And welcome to the home of Robin Hood and his Merry Men.

*All react happily*

Though times have been hard since our beloved King Richard went off to the Crusades, tonight you shall feast in style and enjoy a little rest from the persecution of our old enemy, the Sheriff of Nottingham.

*All agree heartily*

**Alan**  (*calling; good-naturedly*) Never mind the speeches, Tuck. How long before the venison's ready?

*All agree*

**Friar**  (*chuckling*) Well, I'm glad to hear you're hungry, Alan a-Dale. To look at you, a man might think England was in the middle of a famine.

*All laugh*

**Alan**  (*amused*) And to look at you, Father Tuck, he'd think you were the one who'd caused it.

*All laugh even louder*

**Friar**  (*heartily*) If this were not a celebration feast, young bag-o-bones, I'd crack that thick skull of yours with my trusty quarterstaff ——
**All**  Oooooooh ...
**Friar**  — but as I'm a man of peace ——

*All jeer good-naturedly*

— I'll let the insult pass ... providing you pay penance.
**Alan**  (*laughingly*) Penance? And what shall that be, Master Friar?
**Friar**  That you sing for your supper tonight.

*All agree with pleasure*

And not one of your dreamy, dreary ballads, either. Give us a rousing song. Something to put fire in our bellies.

*All agree*

**Alan** Very well, my friends. A song you shall have. And may Prince John hear its words and tremble in his bed at night.

*All cheer loudly*

### Song 11: Alan a-Dale and Company

*At the end of the song, all cheer and applaud*

*Robin enters* UR

**Robin** (*frowning*) Has anyone seen Marion? She should have been here ages ago. (*He moves* DC)
**Will** Perhaps she's having trouble with the Sheriff. (*He grins*) You did make him look a fool this afternoon.

*All agree with smiles and nods*

**Robin** He *is* a fool, Will. But I don't think *he's* the reason. Marion can twist him round her little finger. No. There's something else wrong. I can feel it in my bones.

*Marion hurries on* UL. *She wears a hooded cloak over her gown*

(*Relieved*) Marion. I was starting to worry. You're only just in time.
**Marion** (*hurrying to him*) Oh, Robin. You've got to do something. The Babes have been kidnapped.

*There is a shocked reaction from all*

They vanished from the fairground just after you escaped, and we can't find them anywhere.
**Robin** (*soothingly*) Don't worry, Marion. As soon as we've eaten we'll return to Nottingham and help with the search.
**Marion** But they're not in Nottingham. The villains who took them were followed here ... to Sherwood.
**Robin** Then there's no problem. My men and I know every inch of the forest, and if the Babes are here, then *we'll* find them. Come. By the smell of that venison, it's ready for eating, and we'll be on our way before you know it.

*All exit R deep in conversation*

*As soon as they are gone, Toyle and Trubble enter from L, each holding one of the Babes*

**Toyle** (*moving DC*) Here we are. This'll do.

**Trubble** (*groaning*) Oh, thank goodness for that. My feet are killing me. I've got terrible corns, you know.

**Toyle** Well why don't you put something on 'em?

**Trubble** I have done. I filled my shoes with Corn Flakes, but they don't half crackle when I walk.

*As Toyle reacts, the Babes begin struggling again*

**Jack** Let go of me. Let go.

**Jill** Horrible man.

**Toyle** Oh, all right. We must be in the middle of Sherwood by now.

*The Robbers release the Babes*

But it's no use trying to run away, cos we can run much faster than you can.

**Jill** (*defiantly*) Just you wait till Uncle Cedric finds out what you've done. He'll have you thrown into gaol for ever and ever.

**Toyle** (*amused*) Will he, now? And what would you say if I told you it was Uncle Cedric who's paying us to do this?

**Jack** We wouldn't believe you.

**Toyle** Please yourselves. But as soon as we've done what he's asked us to do, we're gonna be rich. (*He rubs his hands with glee*)

**Jill** (*nervously*) You're not going to hurt us, are you?

**Trubble** (*kindly*) Course not. We wouldn't hurt anybody, us two.

**Jack** Eyes shut, stand on one leg and promise?

**Robbers** (*solemnly*) Eyes shut, stand on one leg and promise.

*They perform the action. Jack and Jill quickly run forward and kick them hard on their supporting legs*

(*Anguished*) Owwwwwww. (*They hop around in pain*)

**Jack** (*to Jill*) Run for it.

*Holding hands, the Babes rush off DL, leaving the Robbers still hopping around*

**Toyle** (*recovering*) That's torn it. If they get back to Nottingham, we'll never get paid. We've got to catch 'em and finish 'em off.

**Trubble** (*startled*) Finish 'em off? You mean, *kill* 'em?

**Toyle** Of course I mean kill 'em, you fathead. We've got to stop 'em talking.

**Trubble** (*indignantly*) I've told you before. I'm killing no kiddies.

**Toyle** (*firmly*) All right, then. I'll kill 'em myself.

**Trubble** Oh, no, you won't. You're not going to lay a finger on 'em.

**Toyle** (*sneering*) And who's going to stop me, then?

**Trubble** (*drawing himself up*) I am.

**Toyle** (*amazed*) You mean you'd fight your old friend ... your oldest and bestest friend ... just to save two miserable little children from getting their scraggy throats cut?

**Trubble** (*defiantly*) Yes.

**Toyle** Well, you rotten thing. (*He draws his pistol*) Very well then. To the death.

**Trubble** To the death. (*He draws his own pistol*)

*They stand back to back, pistols pointing upwards*

**Toyle** Eight paces forward, turn and fire.

*They begin counting loudly. Trubble turns quickly and follows Toyle closely. When they finish counting, Toyle turns smartly to find Trubble's pistol in his face. He screams and tosses his own pistol over his shoulder. Trubble pulls the trigger and a jet of water hits Toyle in the face. Trubble laughs and throws his pistol aside. Quickly they dash off at opposite sides, to re-emerge holding fencing foils*

**Toyle** (*dramatically*) En garde.

**Trubble** (*equally dramatically*) Fire-guard.

*Rushing c, they engage in a swordfight, Trubble holding his foil out at arm's length, perfectly straight, and Toyle's foil describing small circular movements around it. Trubble retreats backwards into the wings, Toyle following until his sword arm is hidden from the audience. He then moves backwards as though driven by Trubble and, gasping and snarling, they both move c before realizing that the two foils have intertwined and are now one solid object. For a moment they vainly try to separate them. Then, tossing the foils aside, they rush off again at opposite sides. They re-emerge clutching swords in scabbards. Toyle draws his sword and flings the scabbard aside, making savage slashing motions with the sword. Trubble draws his weapon and flings the scabbard aside. His weapon is a feather duster fixed to a sword grip*

**Toyle** (*triumphantly*) A-ha.
**Trubble** (*looking at his feather duster in dismay*) Ooo-er.

*Toyle advances on Trubble, and Trubble retreats backwards. Slowly at first, they encircle the glade, then as they pick up speed, Trubble turns and begins to run. Toyle chases him until both are exhausted*

**Toyle** Prepare to die.
**Trubble** (*looking over Toyle's shoulder*) Oh, look. Look.
**Toyle** (*turning round to see*) What?

*Trubble sticks the feather duster between Toyle's legs and jiggles it about. Toyle shrieks with laughter and drops his sword. Trubble scrambles to his feet and dashes off as Toyle recovers and picks up his sword. Trubble rushes on again holding a sword and the two begin a fierce battle. At length, Trubble thrusts his sword between Toyle's body and his upstage arm. Toyle gives a cry and falls to the ground as though dead*

**Trubble** (*uncertainly*) Toyle? Toyle? Come on. Stop messing about. Get up.

*Toyle remains unmoving*

(*Concerned*) Ooooh, I've deaded him. He's kicked the bucket.
**Toyle** (*raising his head*) No, I haven't.
**Trubble** (*upset*) You have. You have. Stop arguing. You're the second man I've killed now. (*He begins sniffling*)
**Toyle** (*sitting up*) Who was the other one?
**Trubble** (*tearfully*) A second-hand car dealer from (*local district*). I reversed right over him and had to bury him the back garden.
**Toyle** Are you sure he was dead?
**Trubble** Well, he kept saying he wasn't, but you know what lies second-hand car dealers tell. (*He bursts into tears again*)
**Toyle** (*getting up*) Oh, stop snivelling. I'm all right. You missed me by a mile. I haven't got a scratch. Look. (*He holds his arms out sideways*)

*Trubble turns and sees him. With a shout of delight he drops his sword, rushes to Toyle, flings his arms round him and plants a big kiss on his cheek. Toyle hurriedly beats him off*

Gerroff. Gerroff. (*He dusts himself down*) Well ... that's that, then. They'll be halfway to Nottingham by now.

**Trubble** Don't care.

**Toyle** And we're never going to get paid.

**Trubble** Still don't care.

**Toyle** (*exasperatedly*) I wasn't *really* going to kill them, you know.

**Trubble** Yes, you were. You wanted those twenty gold pieces.

**Toyle** (*grudgingly*) Well ... maybe I did to start with, but I changed my mind. Honest, I did. I couldn't kill innocent little children, no matter how much I got paid. (*Sadly*) I couldn't kill anybody, really. I'm not a real villain at all. I'm just a great big fraud.

**Trubble** (*ruefully*) Me, too.

**Toyle** (*brightening*) But never mind. We're still friends, aren't we? And no matter what happens now, as long as we've got each other to rely on, we're as good as anybody else in the kingdom.

**Trubble** (*enthusiastically*) You said it.

### Song 12: Toyle and Trubble

*They exit at the end of the song*

*The Lights fade rapidly to a Black-out*

### Scene 4

*A forest path. Evening*

*The Babes enter breathlessly from L and move C*

**Jill** Quick. Quick. (*She tugs at Jack's hand*)

**Jack** (*glancing behind him*) It's all right, Jill. I think we've lost them.

**Jill** (*glancing around*) I think we've lost us, too. And it's getting dark. (*Concerned*) What if we can't find our way home?

**Jack** (*confidently*) Course we can. (*He points off* R) It's just over there. (*Doubtfully*) I think.

**Jill** (*sadly*) Poor Nurse Glucose. She'll be awfully worried about us, won't she?

**Jack** I expect so. But it's all right. We're quite safe now.

**Jill** (*wistfully*) They'll just be sitting down to supper in the castle.

**Jack** (*regretfully*) Yes.

**Jill** (*softly*) I wish we were.

**Jack** Me, too. It seems ages since we had anything to eat.

**Jill** (*miserably*) And it's getting cold, too.
**Jack** (*taking off his jacket*) Here. Wrap this round you.

*He wraps it around her shoulders*

**Jill** (*worried*) They will know we've been kidnapped, won't they? And they will be looking for us?
**Jack** Course they will. It wouldn't surprise me if they were searching the forest right this very minute.
**Jill** (*looking around*) But it's so big and gloomy.
**Jack** Don't worry. They'll find us. I just know they will.

### Song 13: Jack & Jill

*After the song, they move off slowly and exit* R. *As they do so, Nurse Glucose enters from* L, *dragging a reluctant Sheriff behind her*

**Sheriff** (*annoyed*) Wait a minute. Wait a minute. (*He breaks free*) What are we doing in the middle of Sherwood Forest?
**Nurse** Looking for Jack and Jill, of course.
**Sheriff** What? Do you mean to tell me you've dragged me all the way from Nottingham to look for missing children? I'm supposed to be searching for Robin Hood.
**Nurse** (*tartly*) Yes. Well, never mind Robin Hood. He's big enough to look after himself. It's my little Babes I'm worried about.
**Sheriff** Bah. If you ask me, they haven't been kidnapped at all. They've run away to seek their fortune and we'll never see them again.
**Nurse** (*protesting*) But they've already *got* a fortune. Back at the castle. Fifty thousand pounds' worth.
**Sheriff** (*disconcerted*) Oh. Well ... er ... yes. But all the same, I'm sure they've gone for good, so we may as well go back to the castle and make sure the money's still there. (*He begins to exit* L)
**Nurse** (*suspiciously*) Just a minute. Just a minute. You're a bit too eager to get your hands on that money, for my liking. It wouldn't surprise me if you knew more about this than you're telling. (*To the audience*) Do you think he does, girls and boys?

*Audience reaction*

**Sheriff** (*blustering*) You're not going to take any notice of those sycophantic, sanctimonious scruffs, are you? (*To the audience*) Keep your mouths shut or I'll shorten the school holidays.
**Nurse** (*grimly*) You have got something to do with it, haven't you?

**Sheriff**  (*snarling*) You can't prove a thing.

*Robin and Marion enter from* L

**Robin**  (*firmly*) No. But these two can.

*He signals off* L, *and Toyle and Trubble enter, followed by Merry Men, etc.*

**Sheriff**  Curses.

*The Merry Men seize him*

**Robin**  So, friend Sheriff. Your little plan seems to have gone awry. These two villains have confessed everything, and unless I'm much mistaken, as soon as King Richard returns home, Nottingham will see the last of you. (*To the men holding the Sheriff*) Take him away.
**Sheriff**  (*wailing*) No. No. I'm innocent. I've been framed.

*He is dragged off, struggling*

**Nurse**  (*beaming*) So everything's ended happily.
**Marion**  Not quite. We've still to find the Babes. They managed to escape and hide in the forest, and no-one's seen them since.
**Nurse**  (*horrified*) Oh, no.
**Robin**  (*quickly*) Don't worry. We'll have them safe again before you can say Jack Robinson. Marion and I will go this way (*he indicates* R), and the rest of you go that. (*He indicates* L)
**Nurse**  What about me?
**Robin**  I think you'd better wait here and keep an eye on these two. They won't give you any trouble, I can promise. They were only following the Sheriff's orders and seem quite sorry for what they did.
**Toyle**  (*quickly*) Yes, we are.
**Trubble**  Ever so sorry.
**Robin**  (*to the others*) Very well, then. Back to the search.

*Robin and Marion cross to exit* R. *The Merry Men and the others exit* L

*The Lights dim*

**Nurse**  (*nervously*) Oh, I say. It's a bit creepy here now everybody's gone.
**Toyle**  (*bravely*) Don't worry, Nurse Glucose. We'll look after you.

**Trubble** Course we will. (*He glances round*) Here ... but she's right, isn't she? It is creepy. If you ask me, this place could be haunted.
**Nurse** (*nervously*) Haunted?
**Toyle** (*scornfully*) Don't be daft. There's no such thing as ghosts.
**Nurse** Oh, yes there is. I stayed in a haunted house once, and at three o'clock in the morning, a ghost came through the wall just as though there were no wall there at all.
**Trubble** (*wide-eyed*) And what did you do?
**Nurse** I went through the opposite wall, the same way.
**Toyle** Well ... what if there *is* a ghost round here? It can't frighten us.
**Trubble** Can't it?
**Toyle** Course it can't. Because I've heard that ghosts are scared of music, so if we have a little singsong, it won't dare come near us.
**Nurse** (*impressed*) Oh, I say. Well, let's sing something, then.
**Trubble** Ah, yes ... but what if we're singing, and it creeps up behind us?
**Toyle** Easy. We ask all the girls and boys in the audience to shout out and warn us. (*To the audience*) Will you do that, kids?

*Audience reaction*

**Nurse** (*beaming*) Oh, lovely. So what shall we sing?
**Trubble** How about "She Left Her Electric Blanket on, and Now She's the Toast of the Town"?
**Toyle** No, no, no. We can't sing that. Nobody knows the words. I'll tell you what. We'll sing (*he names the song*), cos we all know that one.

### Song 14: Nurse, Toyle and Trubble

*They begin to sing*

*After two lines, a Ghost enters from* L, *flits behind them and exits* R

*As the audience react, the singing wavers and fades*

**Nurse** (*to Toyle*) What's the matter? What's the matter? Why are they shouting?
**Trubble** They say there's a ghost behind us.

*Toyle and Nurse react*

**Toyle** (*glancing round, cautiously*) I can't see anything.
**Nurse** (*warily*) Neither can I, but let's have a proper look.

*With great stealth, they tiptoe around until they have completed a circle
and are back in their original positions*

**Trubble** There's nothing there at all. They're having us on.
**Toyle** (*to the audience*) Rotten things. (*To others*) Let's carry on singing.

*The singing begins again*

   *The Ghost enters from R, crosses behind them and exits L*

*As the audience react, the singing stops again*

**Nurse** What's wrong now?
**Trubble** They say it came back again.
**Toyle** (*to audience*) Oh, no it didn't.

*Audience reaction*

**Nurse** I think we'd better have another look.

*The others agree, and they circle anti-clockwise until they are in their
original positions again*

**Toyle** Nothing there at all. Not a sausage.
**Trubble** Let's carry on singing.

*They sing again*

   *The Ghost enters from R and taps Trubble on the shoulder. He looks
   round, sees it, reacts, and dashes off L, chased by the Ghost*

*The others sing on until they realize he is gone*

**Nurse** Oh, I say. He's gone. Done a bunk. Dashed off.
**Toyle** Must have been the curry he had last night.
**Nurse** Vindaloo?
**Toyle** No, but I think he's just going.

*They begin to sing again*

   *The Ghost enters from L and taps Toyle on the shoulder. He turns, sees
   it, reacts and dashes off R, chased by the Ghost*

*Nurse notices he has vanished and stops singing*

**Nurse** Oh, dear. He's gone as well. Left me all alone. By meself. With nobody with me. (*She shrugs*) Oh, well, I suppose I can sing on my own. After all ... I was going to be a professional singer until I had throat trouble. The neighbours threatened to cut it. (*She begins to sing*)

*The Ghost enters and taps her on the shoulder*

*She turns*

*The Ghost screams and exits*

*Black-out*

SCENE 5

*Deep in Sherwood Forest. Night*

*A large clearing with a small grassy hummock upstage. (This can be the same set as Scene 3 with the hummock added, if resources are limited)*

*Jack and Jill enter wearily* UL

**Jill** It's no use, Jack. I can't walk another step.
**Jack** Nor me. And I'm sure we're walking in circles. (*He yawns*) Oh, I'm so tired. Let's lie down over here ... (*he indicates the hummock*) and try to sleep. We'll find our way much easier when it's daylight. (*He moves towards the hummock*)
**Jill** (*following him*) But what about wild animals?
**Jack** Oh, I'm sure they won't hurt us. Besides ... I'm too tired to care. (*He yawns again*)

*They sit on the hummock*

**Jill** (*timidly*) Will we ever see Nurse Glucose and Marion again, Jack?
**Jack** (*sleepily*) Of course we will. And as soon as they hear how Uncle Cedric had us kidnapped, they'll have him thrown into his own dungeons. (*He yawns*) Good-night, Jill. (*He settles down on the hummock*)
**Jill** Good-night, Jack. (*She snuggles down beside him*)

*The Lights dim. After a moment, the Fairy enters* DR

**Fairy** (*to Babes*) Sleep tight until the night is spent.
You're safe at last from cruel intent.
(*To the audience*) With leafy blankets I'll adorn
These Babes to keep them snug and warm,
Whilst pleasant dreams erase their sorrow
'Til they are found upon the morrow.

(*She waves her wand*)

Come forest birds, there's work to do
The Forest Fairy summons you.

*She exits* R

*The Birds enter carrying an assortment of leaves which they gently place over the sleeping Babes until they are covered. This should be done as the Birds perform a stylish dance in lullaby tempo*

### Dance: Birds of the Forest

*At the end of the dance, the Birds exit*

*The Lights come up as morning dawns*

*Marion's voice is heard off* L

**Marion** (*calling*) Children? Children?

*The Merry Men appear upstage, searching. Robin Hood enters* DR

**Robin** Jack? Jill? Can you hear me?

*The Babes sit up*

**Jack** Robin Hood.
**Jill** We're here. We're here!

*The Babes scramble up as Robin hurries to them*

**Robin** (*calling*) Over here. I've found them.

*Merry Men hurry forward*

*Friar Tuck enters* DL, *holding the Sheriff, who is in handcuffs. Marion and Nurse enter* UL

**Marion** (*hurrying to the Babes*) Oh, thank goodness. We were so worried about you. (*She hugs them*)
**Nurse** (*tearfully*) My little Babes. (*She hugs them*)
**Robin** The only trouble is ... now that we've found them, what do we do with them? They can't go back to live at the castle if the Sheriff's in gaol.

*The Fairy enters* R

**Nurse** (*startled*) Good heavens. It's ... (*well-known female TV character*)!
**Robin** (*awed*) The Forest Fairy.

*At once Robin and the Merry Men kneel and bow their heads. Only Marion, Nurse, the Sheriff and Babes remain standing*

**Fairy** Good tidings now, dear friends, I bring
To England's shores, returns the King.

*All but the Sheriff react excitedly*

Who vows, "Those wronged in Prince John's reign,
Their lands and titles will regain."
Which means ... bold Robin shall become
Once more, the Earl of Huntingdon.

*All but the Sheriff cheer in delight and rise*

**Robin** (*happily*) Then Marion and I shall be married at once ——

*She hurries to him*

—— and the Babes will live with us at Lockesley Hall.
**Jack** But what about Nurse Glucose?
**Jill** We can't leave her behind.
**Nurse** (*beaming*) Oh, don't worry about me, dears. I won't be far away. I'm going to open my own little chemist shop in Nottingham, and as soon as Uncle Cedric gets out of gaol, he's coming to work for me ... as Chief Castor Oil Taster. (*She chortles*)

*Everyone but the Sheriff looks amused*

**Sheriff** (*anguished*) No. Noooooo. Mercy ...
**Robin** (*declaiming*) So back to Nottingham without delay,
          To prepare our joyous wedding day.

*All cheer*

### Song 15: Robin and Company

*At the end of the song the Lights fade rapidly to Black-out*

SCENE 6

*Back in Nottingham*

*The Lights come up to full*

*Toyle and Trubble enter in finale costumes*

**Toyle** Cor. Isn't it smashing to be clean and well-dressed and so full you
          couldn't eat another thing?
**Trubble** Not half. And now we've been forgiven for doing the Sheriff's
          dirty work, we've even got jobs as well.
**Toyle** (*frowning*) Yes. And I suppose we'd better make a start, hadn't
          we? It won't be long before the wedding.
**Trubble** Here ... (*he glances at the audience*) I wonder if that lot'd help?
**Toyle** (*looking doubtfully at audience*) Oooh, I shouldn't think so.(*He
          reconsiders*) Mind you ... there's a lot of them, isn't there? I mean, they
          should be able to make a noise.
**Trubble** Course they should. I can see one woman down there with a
          mouth as big as a ——

*Toyle quickly claps his hand over Trubble's mouth*

**Toyle** (*tightly*) Let's ask 'em, then, shall we? (*Pointedly*) Politely.
**Trubble** Oh, all right. (*To the audience*) Er ... sorry to bother you, but
          we've just been given the job of finding a choir for Robin and Marion's
          wedding ... and we wondered if you'd like to help?

*Audience reaction*

**Toyle** (*pleased*) You would? Smashing. Well, I'm sure you'll all know the words, so we'll sing it through first, then you sing it the second time. All right?

*The Song Sheet begins. The Robbers conduct the proceedings as required*

*At the end they exit quickly*

*The Lights fade to Black-out*

### SCENE 7

*Lockesley Hall and Finale. A splendid medieval hall. Full lighting*

*Dancers perform a lively dance*

### Dance: Dancers

*They quickly exit as the finale walkdown begins, in this order:*

*Juniors*
*Citizens and Merry Men*
*Bailiff*
*Alan a-Dale*
*Friar Tuck, Will Scarlett and Much*
*Fairy*
*Sheriff*
*Jack and Jill*
*Toyle and Trubble*
*Nurse Glucose*
*Robin and Marion*

**Robin** Our pantomime is over. This merry tale is done.
**Marion** We hope you've all enjoyed these hours of music, dance and fun.
**Toyle** As an audience, you've been perfect,
**Trubble** Or at least ... extremely good.
**Nurse** So till we meet again, *good-night*, from all of us ——
**All** In *The Babes in the Wood*!

### Song 16: Company

*There is a reprise of the walkdown number which everyone sings*

### CURTAIN

# FURNITURE AND PROPERTY LIST

## ACT I
### SCENE 1

*On stage:*     Nil

*Off stage:*    Rolled scroll (**Sheriff**)
Luggage, packages, umbrella, etc. (**Nurse**)
Large envelope with letter (**Marion**)
Large money bag (**Babes**)

*Personal:*     **Toyle:** pistol
**Trubble:** pistol

### SCENE 2

No props required

### SCENE 3

*On stage:*     Teacher's desk
3 dunce's caps
Cane
Blackboard on easel
Nail
Chalks
Eraser
2 long benches
1 shorter bench with legs missing from one side
Conkers
Paper darts

*Off stage:*    Large apple (**Toyle**)

*Personal:*     **Nurse:** cap, gown, large handbell

### SCENE 4

*On stage:*     Nil

| *Off stage:* | Lantern (**Marion**) |
| | Lantern (**Friar Tuck**) |
| | Bow and arrows (**Robin**) |

## SCENE 5

| *On stage:* | Large bed with bedclothes |
| | Bedside table |
| | Rocking chair |
| | Thick fairy story book |
| | Toys |

| *Off stage:* | Large bottle of castor oil (**Nurse**) |
| | Ladle (**Nurse**) |

## ACT II
### SCENE 1

| *On stage:* | Nil |

| *Off stage:* | Velvet cushion with golden arrow (**Bailiff**) |
| | Bows and arrows (**Will Scarlett, Much** and **Robin Hood**) |

| *Personal:* | **Trubble:** small bottle (in pocket) |
| | **Nurse:** arrow (in bustle) |

## SCENE 2

| *On stage:* | Nil |

| *Off stage:* | Handkerchief (**Nurse**) |

## SCENE 3

| *On stage:* | Nil |

| *Off stage:* | 2 fencing foils (**Toyle** and **Trubble**) |
| | 2 intertwined foils (**Toyle** and **Trubble**) |
| | Sword in scabbard (**Toyle**) |
| | Feather duster on sword grip in scabbard (**Trubble**) |
| | Sword (**Trubble**) |

| *Personal:* | **Toyle:** pistol |
| | **Trubble:** water pistol |

SCENE 4

*On stage:*      Nil

SCENE 5

*On stage:*      Hummock

*Off stage:*     Leaves (**Birds**)

*Personal:*      **Sheriff:** handcuffs

SCENE 6

*On stage:*      Nil

SCENE 7

*On stage:*      Nil

# LIGHTING PLOT

Interior and exterior settings
Practical fittings required: 2 lanterns for Act I, Scene 4

ACT I, SCENE 1   Exterior
*To open:*   Bring up bright sunlight effect

*Cue* 1        The **Sheriff** exits                                                (Page 13)
             *Fade and bring up white spot on* **Fairy** DR

*Cue* 2        The **Fairy** exits                                                 (Page 13)
             *Cut spot and fade to black-out*

ACT I, SCENE 2   Exterior
*To open:*   Bring up daylight effect

*Cue* 3        **Marion** and the **Babes** exit                              (Page 17)
             *Fade quickly to black-out*

ACT I, SCENE 3   Schoolroom
*To open:*   Bring up interior day effect

*No cues*

ACT I, SCENE 4   Exterior
*To open:*   Change to exterior evening effect

*Cue* 4        All exit L after Song 5                                      (Page 28)
             *Bring up white spot on* **Fairy** R

*Cue* 5        **Fairy:** "... the night to keep."                           (Page 28)
             *Black-out*

ACT I, SCENE 5   Bedroom
*To open:*   Bring up interior evening effect

*Cue* 6        **Nurse:** "... there'll be much doing."                      (Page 33)
             *Dim; bring up spot on* **Fairy** DR

| *Cue* 7 | **Fairy** exits | (Page 34) |
| | *Cut spot* | |

| *Cue* 8 | **Nurse:** "Nighty-night, dears. Nighty-night." | (Page 34) |
| | *Dim further* | |

| *Cue* 9 | **Babes** enter and watch in dismay | (Page 35) |
| | *Black-out* | |

ACT II, SCENE 1     Exterior
*To open:*   Bring up bright daylight effect

| *Cue* 10 | **Nurse:** "Help. Help!" | (Page 42) |
| | *Fade rapidly to black-out* | |

ACT II, SCENE 2     Exterior
*To open:*   Bring up daylight effect

| *Cue* 11 | The **Sheriff** escorts **Nurse** off L | (Page 44) |
| | *Fade; bring up white spot R on* **Fairy** | |

| *Cue* 12 | The **Fairy** exits | (Page 44) |
| | *Black-out* | |

ACT II, SCENE 3     Exterior
*To open:*   Bring up forest effect, early evening

| *Cue* 13 | **Toyle** and **Trubble** exit | (Page 50) |
| | *Fade rapidly to black-out* | |

ACT II, SCENE 4     Exterior
*To open:*   Bring up forest effect, evening

| *Cue* 14 | **Robin, Marion, Merry Men** and others exit | (Page 52) |
| | *Dim slightly* | |

| *Cue* 15 | The **Ghost** screams and exits | (Page 55) |
| | *Black-out* | |

ACT II, SCENE 5     Exterior
*To open:*   Bring up deep forest effect, night

| *Cue* 16 | **Jill:** "Good-night, Jack." | (Page 55) |
| | *Dim slightly* | |

*Cue* 17     The **Birds** exit                                          (Page 56)
             *Bring up dawn effect*

*Cue* 18     Song 15 ends                                                (Page 58)
             *Fade rapidly to black-out*

ACT II, Scene 6     Exterior
*To open:*    Bring up general exterior effect

*Cue* 19     **Toyle** and **Trubble** exit                              (Page 59)
             *Fade to black-out*

ACT II, Scene 7     Interior
*To open:*    Bring up full interior lighting

*No cues*

# EFFECTS PLOT

## ACT I

*Cue* 1    **Nurse** tosses the invisible cup aside                    (Page 34)
           *After a moment, sound of a cup breaking*

## ACT II

*Cue* 2    **Toyle:** "Where does your girlfriend live?"             (Page 39)
           *Fanfare*